# Pilgrims *in* Progress

*Growing through Groups*

## Jim & Carol Plueddemann

Harold Shaw Publishers
Wheaton, Illinois

ISBN 0-87788-647-4

Cover illustration: Roberta Polfus

Library of Congress Cataloging-in-Publication Data

Plueddemann, Jim.
    Pilgrims in progress: growing through groups / Jim and Carol Plueddemann.
        p.    cm.
    Includes bibliographical references.
    ISBN 0-87788-647-4
    1. Church group work. I. Plueddemann, Carol. II. Title.
BV652.2.P555    1990
267'.1—dc20                                          89-49279
                                                      CIP

99  98  97  96  95  94

10  9  8  7  6  5  4  3  2

*Dedicated to our fathers,*
*Edwin P. Plueddemann*
*and*
*Robert C. Savage*
*(1914-1987),*
*faithful pilgrims who pointed us to the Path*
*and continue to cheer us toward our Goal*
(Hebrews 12:1)

# Contents

Blessed are those whose strength is in you,
who have **set their hearts on pilgrimage.**
They go from strength to strength,
till each appears before God in Zion.

*Psalm 84:5, 7*

# Pilgrims of Eternity

*God of my forefathers . . . I thank Thee
that this Christian way whereon I walk
is no untried or uncharted road,
but a road beaten hard by the footsteps
of saints, apostles, prophets, and martyrs.
I thank Thee for the finger-posts and danger-signals
with which it is marked at every turning.*
JOHN BAILLIE, A Diary of Private Prayer

CHRIST HAS CALLED US TO A JOURNEY—A JOURNEY THAT CAN'T BE traveled alone. Pilgrims need other pilgrims. The road is long, days are hot, and nights are cold. The journey is contested every yard of the way with conflict and temptation. There is weariness, pain, hunger, poverty, and danger—even darkness and death.

Pilgrims travel with little baggage, depending on help from other pilgrims along the way. They need a map, and they also need assistance in interpreting the map. Pilgrims long for advice from those who have traveled the road ahead. Close relationships are important. But warm feelings are not enough—there is a journey to be run, and a destination to reach. An authoritative Map points the way.

There are also rewards, both along the way and at the journey's end. John Bunyan's *Pilgrim's Progress* clearly pictures the unrelenting struggle faced by Christian, but Bunyan also shows the pilgrim walk as one of transcendent joy. There is singing, communion, beauty, and encouragement. And finally, there is the eternal delight of meeting God and praising him forever.

How can pilgrims encourage each other most effectively? Small groups can be seen as bands of pilgrims, helping each other on their journey from this world to the next. This is a book about why small groups work and how they can be most effective.

# 1

# Pilgrim Groups in Historical Perspective

*The use of small groups of one kind or another
seems to be a common element
in all significant movements
of the Holy Spirit throughout church history.*
HOWARD A. SNYDER, The Problem of Wineskins

$S$OME PEOPLE ENTHUSIASTICALLY POINT TO SMALL GROUPS AS
*the* way for pilgrims to grow in faith. Others suspiciously view
small groups as a modern fad with all kinds of problems. Setting
small groups in a historical context can help us understand both
their benefits and their potential problems.

## Small Groups in the Old Testament

The Old Testament shows God at work in family groupings and
other forms of small groups to accomplish his covenant purposes.
When God delivered his chosen people from the slavery of Egypt,
he could have taken them directly to the Promised Land. The
distance from Egypt to Palestine was shorter than the miles from
Philadelphia to New York. But God's purposes included far more
than getting from one place to another. Taking the people out of

Egypt was much easier than taking Egypt out of the people! And so a journey that could have been completed in a week of comfortable travel became a forty-year pilgrimage. During this journey, Jethro suggested that Moses divide the people into groups of tens, fifties, hundreds, and thousands. This division into larger and smaller groups helped Moses and the other leaders to care for the needs of the people in a better way.

The people of God were referred to as "the children of Israel." Family-oriented metaphors are sprinkled throughout the Old Testament to describe God's relationship with his people. The home was the center of religious instruction, emphasizing this family relationship with God. The Passover Feast was held in households, either one large household or several smaller ones together. This intimate setting fostered the opportunity for children to ask the meaning of the feast and so had important pedagogical as well as symbolic implications.

Of course there were also times when the people of Israel gathered in large assemblies to hear the Law of the Lord. Nehemiah 8 describes one such occasion when Ezra read the Book of the Law while the Levites helped him explain the meaning to the people so they could understand what was being read. This seems to have been a combination of large group and small group teaching. Throughout the Old Testament, God used a variety of large and small group settings to meet the needs of his people and to equip them for carrying out his purposes.

## Jesus' Small Group

Jesus chose a small group of twelve to be with him, to learn from him, and to minister with him. The formation of this group was not an afterthought in Jesus' ministry—he spent a night in prayer before choosing The Twelve (Luke 6:12-16). Within this group of twelve, three ministered even more intimately to and with Jesus.

Jesus needed a small group. He allowed others to minister to him, however faltering and imperfect their ministry was. And Jesus made optimum use of the small group as an effective educational setting to help his disciples learn and grow.

## Small Groups in the Early Church

Following Jesus' ascension, the disciples continued to put into practice what they had learned in their small group with Jesus. After Peter's Pentecost sermon, the church grew explosively from 120 people (Acts 1:15) to over 3,000 people (Acts 2:41). How would these new believers grow in their faith to become mature Christians? Acts 2 describes a two-prong pattern of believers gathering in large group meetings and in small home groups:

> They devoted themselves to the apostles' teaching and to the fellowship, to the breaking of bread and to prayer. Everyone was filled with awe, and many wonders and miraculous signs were done by the apostles. All the believers were together and had everything in common. Selling their possessions and goods, they gave to anyone as he had need. Every day they continued to meet together in the temple courts. They broke bread in their homes and ate together with glad and sincere hearts, praising God and enjoying the favor of all the people. And the Lord added to their number daily those who were being saved. *Acts 2:42-46*

The small groups in homes complemented the large group meetings held in the temple courts. Rather than competing, each format provided essential elements to the believers' growth. In addition to the worship and teaching of the central gatherings, the home groups provided nurture, fellowship, prayer, and outreach opportunities. The result? Believers who were devoted to Scripture and its outworking in their lives. In addition, the church grew numerically—"The Lord added to their number daily those who were being saved."

The New Testament church was a community of faith, the assembled family of God. Paul called it "God's household" (1 Tim. 3:15). This was a reflection of the church's Old Testament roots where the people of God are described as his family, his children. The small group setting, then, was a natural expression of the nature of the church itself.

Home gatherings are continually mentioned in the New Testament as settings for God's work. On the Day of Pentecost, the believers were gathered in a home when the Holy Spirit came like the rush of a mighty wind and "filled the whole house where they were sitting" (Acts 2:2). It was in the home of Cornelius, a Roman centurion, where Peter first brought the gospel to the Gentiles.

All of the New Testament churches that are designated as having specific locations were in homes. There was a house church in the home of Priscilla and Aquila. Paul commended them in Romans 16 and said, "Greet also the church that meets at their house." Paul also sent special greetings "to Nympha and the church in her house" (Col. 4:15). Another church group met in the home of Philemon. Paul sent greetings "to Philemon our dear friend and fellow worker . . . and to the church that meets in your home." These home gatherings complemented the meetings held in the temple and the synagogues, providing a dynamic expression of church family life.

### Fourth Century

A significant change took place during the fourth century with the legitimization of Christianity under Constantine. Previously, because Christianity had been an illegal religion and worship often had to be in secret, the church was largely home-based. But now that the emperor had officially embraced Christianity, church structures replaced house churches.

Some see this era as "the triumph of the church" that ensured the preservation of Christianity. Others view it as "the fall of the church" because the church became institutionalized and vulnerable to political corruption. Elements of both views probably represent the realities of the situation. At any rate, the focus of the church changed from home gatherings to church structures. The basilica emerged as a church architectural form, featuring a rectangular hall and a semicircular niche with a thronelike chair for the bishop.[1] The basilica was the forerunner of the cathedral and symbolized a qualitatively different direction for the church.

> Worship changed from being the united celebration of all the people to a clergy-performed ritual with the laity as spectators. It was a fundamental departure. . . . This building-centered structure of the church has dominated institutional church life ever since.[2]

The priesthood of all believers was de-emphasized and believers no longer gathered together in homes as before.

> Worship in the house church had been of an intimate kind in which all present had taken an active part. But by the beginning of the fourth century, the distinction between clergy and lay people was becoming more prominent. . . . The liturgy changed from being a corporate action of the whole church into a service said by the clergy to which the laity listened.[3]

The bishop, who had previously focused on pastoral and spiritual concerns, now assumed additional administrative duties. Control of finances and personnel often became an exercise in political power. Many believe that the church was weakened by this trend.

Monastic movements, such as those of Benedict and Augustine, continued to gather men and women into intentional communities for growth in faith and expressions of service. But unlike the house churches, monasticism had no room for the family. Christian instruction in homes continued, but it no longer had an integral connection with church life.

**The Reformation**

Historically, a reinstitution of the use of small groups has accompanied almost every recorded revival. According to J. Edwin Orr,

> Just before the fifteenth century something started to change the church. It resulted in a progression of spiritual awakenings in which small groups either spearheaded, became strong catalysts of, or followed as nurturing environments to revivals.[4]

The Protestant Reformation of the sixteenth century again emphasized the priesthood of all believers. With Martin Luther's new translation of the Bible, Scripture was available for personal and group study. At one point, Luther expressed a vision of the devout meeting in homes "to pray, to read, to baptize, to receive the sacrament, and to do other Christian works. . . . Here one could set up a brief and neat order for baptism and the sacrament and center everything on the Word, prayer, and love." This vision did not materialize, however, "because I have not yet the people or persons for it, nor do I see many who want it."[5]

During this era, the house church was associated with the more radical wing of the Reformation, especially the Anabaptists. The Anabaptists had no church buildings but met in homes several times a week for worship and nurture. This may have been partly because of the persecution they experienced from Lutherans, Calvinists, and Catholics combined. But Durnbaugh points out that even when persecution let up, they preferred to meet in homes because this was more faithful to the practice of the early church.[6]

## Post-Reformation Period

In the post-Reformation period, the Church of the Brethren continued the pattern of house-church worship, inspired by the Anabaptists.[7]

Within the Pietist movement of the seventeenth and eighteenth centuries, Philip Jacob Spener and August Hermann Francke started house meetings for prayer, Bible study, and discussion. Spener wrote about the "little church within the church," which he saw as a means of renewal for a rigid and dogmatic church establishment. Each week Spener brought the parishoners together to talk about the sermon, giving them opportunities to ask questions and to contribute their own insights. A significant feature of these home meetings is that women were included and encouraged to participate with questions and insights.[8]

Count Zinzendorf, founder of the Moravian movement, was tutored by Francke in his home school. Zinzendorf, in turn, profoundly influenced John Wesley and William Carey. As a student, Zinzendorf had a passion to know Jesus Christ and to make him known to others. With five others, he formed the Order of the Grain of Mustard Seed. They were bound together in prayer for the purpose of witnessing to the power of Christ. The worldwide missionary movement of the Moravians was born in the hearts of this group of students who joined together to pray for world evangelism.[9] As the movement spread, the converts were gathered into house groups.

Many say that John Wesley's eighteenth-century revival flourished because he organized the converts into groups of ten, each with its own leaders.[10] Neighborhood class meetings held in homes were the cornerstone of Wesley's methodology. These home groups met important needs for people who were experiencing the upheaval of the Industrial Revolution in England. Hundreds of thousands of people participated in these small class meetings in a movement that eventually crossed two continents and two different cultures.[11] The majority of leaders in Wesley's class meetings were women. His own mother, Susannah, had initiated home meetings in the parsonage years before. These began with devotional times which Susannah led for her children. A few neighbors asked to attend, and eventually the group grew to over 200 people.[12] This venture eventually came to an end because of opposition from Susannah's husband and other church leaders, but the vision for home groups would become an important dynamic in the ministry of her sons, John and Charles.

The famous "haystack prayer meeting" of 1806 grew out of a student prayer group led by Samuel J. Mills, Jr. This group met regularly to pray for the spiritual welfare of their fellow students. Their haystack prayer meeting focused on the awakening of foreign missionary interest among students and led to the first student missionary society in America. This society provided the main impulse for the foreign missionary movement of American churches.[13]

Home meetings continued to be an important part of the Wesleyan tradition and the holiness movement that grew out of it. Phoebe Palmer was an important figure in that movement in America during the nineteenth century. The famous "Tuesday Meeting for the Promotion of Holiness" met in her home from 1839 until her death in 1874. The meetings were attended by bishops and notable society people as well as common people.[14]

The coming together of Christians in homes has a long-standing tradition in Christian history. As Hadaway, Wright, and DuBose point out,

Most modern denominations had their origin in house meetings. This was true of the Baptists and Disciples as well as the

Methodists. The Holiness revival that swept the United States the latter part of the nineteenth century and the modern Pentecostal movement which began in the early part of this century had their genesis in home meetings.[15]

## The Modern Period

The major development of the small group movement in the modern period has taken place in the second half of this century. This development can be seen around the globe. Great Britain began to experience the "home church movement" toward the end of World War II. In South America, "base communities" have sprung up within the Roman Catholic Church, with over eighty thousand such groups in Brazil alone.[16] These are lay-oriented and are essentially a response to concern for the poor.

One of the most astounding manifestations of home churches has been in mainland China. When diplomatic relations were first restored with China, Christians wondered if any believers had survived the Cultural Revolution. What they found was a church far stronger than before the communist take-over of 1949—held together by thousands of house churches. These house churches survived and grew throughout the Cultural Revolution, in spite of persecution. The parallel to the first-century Christians who suffered and thrived under persecution by the Roman Empire is significant. Today there are thousands of house churches in China, attended by millions of Chinese.[17] This movement is being threatened by the reorganization of the government-sanctioned Three-Self Movement churches. A number of house church leaders have been arrested as China seeks to regain control of the church.

The Full Gospel Central Church of Seoul, Korea has become the largest church in the world, with over half-a-million members. This growth has come about largely through the development of home cell groups. Fifty thousand such groups were reported by that church in 1987.[18] Thousands of pastors have studied and adopted cell group strategy as outlined by Paul Yonggi Cho in his book *Successful Home Cell Groups*.[19] Cho's church has a significant place for women as home cell leaders. Approximately two-thirds of the cell leaders are women.

The church in America "re-discovered" small groups in the 1950s and '60s. Earlier, in the 1930s, the scientific study of groups emerged at Kurt Lewin's Research Center for Group Dynamics as social science researchers recognized the unique outcomes that take place in small group settings. Church leaders began to take a strong interest in the potential for small groups in ministry.

Lyman Coleman, one of the modern pioneers of the small group movement in the church, describes each of the last four decades with the following summary:

**The '50s:**
"The Age of the Prophets"—the birth of the movement.
The model: Covenant groups
The emphasis: Bible study

**The '60s:**
"The Age of the Activists"—the idealists take over.
The model: Mission/Action groups
The emphasis: Social concern

**The '70s:**
"The Age of the Fadists"—the movement goes pop.
The model: Growth groups
The emphasis: Self-fulfillment and support

**The '80s:**
"The Age of Integration"—church growth enters the picture.
The model: Assimilation groups
The emphasis: Balance between Bible study, mission, and support[20]

The past three decades have seen a proliferation of all kinds of home-based groups. As Coleman indicates in his summary, there have been pendulum swings and varied emphases. Some groups and house churches were formed as a reaction against institutionalized churches. This was part of the counterculture movement of the late 1960s and early 1970s. Many forms emerged, some with cultic characteristics. Other groups met with a sincere desire for a deeper expression of Christianity. But the excesses of certain groups caused the whole movement to be suspect in some circles. Though there are still problems and dangers connected with some home-based groups, there seems to be a better understanding of both the benefits and the pitfalls of small groups today that is leading to a healthier approach.

Whereas most of the small group movement of the '60s and early '70s took place outside of church structures and even in reaction to the institutional church, today that picture has changed dramatically. Small group ministries are proliferating within the church and as outreaches from the church. Many pastors and congregations are intentionally developing a variety of small group ministries as the core of their church life.

## The Future of Small Groups

Is the small group movement here to stay?

Every movement is, to some extent, a product of its culture and reflects the problems and issues that face society. Our age, even more than John Bunyan's, looms as a trackless wasteland. Roads seem to lead nowhere, if they can be found at all. People are looking for a clear way through the wilderness of our modern world. The postwar generation of the fifties and sixties was the first to grow up in an urban, technical society with its complexities of mass communications, computer dominance, and fear of nuclear holocaust. This is the same generation that is desperately seeking a return to community and forming the nucleus of the small group movement.

Speaking of the baby boomer generation, Paula Rinehart says,

The challenge before this generation is to reconcile two conflict-
ing desires: on one hand, the hunger for self-fulfillment, and on
the other, the longing for community and a wider impact upon
the world around them. The message of the gospel presents the
only real hope for the fulfillment of both desires. It does this by
enabling the individual to find meaning and community as he
or she participates in the larger purposes of God.[21]

In his book *New Rules*, Daniel Yankelovich highlights surveys
that indicate concern for community has increased among young
Americans. In addition, many speak more openly about their
religious beliefs and concern for the future.[22]

John Naisbitt, author of *Megatrends*, suggests that one of the
major forces emerging in contemporary society is the widespread
preference for decentralization in most social and political institu-
tions.[23] The small group movement is a reflection of this larger
trend in society.

Since small group ministries are a response to needs in our
society and since they have strong roots in history, it is likely that
they are an enduring structure. How, then, can we encourage the
healthy practice of small groups? The key is a biblically based
philosophy that asks important questions about our ultimate purpose in life, about the nature of persons, and about aims and
methodologies. That's what this book is all about.

### Questions for Reflection

1. In what ways do you think home groups contributed to the
vitality of the early church? What other factors might have contributed to its strength?

2. What factors in our society today contribute to individualism? To community?

3. Do you see the use of small groups in ministry as a passing fad or as an ongoing need?

### Notes

1. See *Eerdmans' Handbook to the History of Christianity*, Tim Dowley, ed. (Grand Rapids: Eerdmans Publishing Co., 1977), pp. 150-52 for a description of the basilica along with photographs and illustrations.

2. C. Kirk Hadaway, Stuart A. Wright, and Francis M. Dubose, *Home Cell Groups and House Churches* (Nashville: Broadman Press, 1987), p. 71.

3. Henry R. Sefton, "Building for Worship" in *Eerdmans' Handbook to the History of Christianity*, ed. by Dowley, p. 151.

4. Quoted in Karen Hurston, "Home Groups: Channels for Growth," *Ministries Today*, May/June, 1987, p. 67.

5. Martin Luther, "The German Mass and Order of Service," *Luther's Works*, Volume 53, edited by Ulrich S. Leupold (Philadelphia: Fortress Press, 1965), pp. 63-64.

6. Donald F. Durnbaugh, "Intentional Community in Historical Perspective," *The House Church Evolving*, ed. Arthur L. Foster (Chicago: Exploration Press, 1976), p. 18.

7. Ibid, p. 17.

8. Ibid, pp. 19-20.

9. David M. Howard, *Student Power in World Missions* (Downers Grove, Ill.: InterVarsity Press, 1979) p. 65.

10. See Howard A. Snyder, *The Radical Wesley and Patterns for Church Renewal* (Downers Grove, Ill.: Inter Varsity Press, 1980). Snyder also describes the Anglican religious societies that pre-dated Wesley and that became a mini-renewal element in the early 1700s (pp. 14-18).

11. See James A. Davies, "Small Groups: Are They Really So New?" *Christian Education Journal*, Volume V, Number 2 (Fall, 1984) for a helpful description of Wesley's class meetings and their implications for small groups today.

12.  Snyder, pp. 16-18.

13.  Howard, p. 75.

14.  Grant Wacker, "The Entire Sanctification of an Extraordinary Ego," *Christianity Today*, October 6, 1989, p. 56.

15.  Hadaway, et. al., p. 50.

16.  Hurston, p. 67.

17.  Anthony P. B. Lambert, "Counting Christians in China: Who's Right?" *News Network International*, April 14, 1989.

18.  Hadaway, et al., p. 80.

19.  Paul Yonggi Cho, *Successful Home Cell Groups* (Plainfield, N.J.: Bridge Publishing, Inc., 1981).

20.  Lyman Coleman, *Training Manual for Small Group Leaders* (Littleton, Co.: Serendipity House, 1987), pp. 32-33.

21.  Paula Rinehart, "The Pivotal Generation," *Christianity Today*, October 6, 1989, p. 27.

22.  Daniel Yankelovich, *New Rules: Searching for Self-Fulfillment in a World Turned Upside Down* (New York: Bantam, 1981), pp. 9-10.

23.  John Naisbitt, *Megatrends: Ten New Directions Transforming Our Lives* (New York: Warner, 1982), pp. 97-130.

## *Why Small Groups Are Important to Me*

While at Ntare School in my first year of high school, I was introduced to a small Scripture Union group. I was not a born-again Christian, though I had cynically attended church in earlier years. I became a Christian through the ministry of these brothers in the high school group. They introduced me to small group Bible study where the theme was "read your Bible and pray every day if you want to grow." Scripture Union encouraged individual study, small group study, and growth through larger group conferences. There was a four-way focus in each of these settings—nurture, fellowship, prayer, and witness. The Bible was at the heart of all these activities.

My biggest spiritual breakthroughs have been in small groups. I've experienced significant growth by struggling in a diverse group. Diversity can cause tremendous tension, but it also fosters great growth. The non-Christians who attended one lunch-hour group sharpened our thinking and broke us out of our clichés. Some became Christians—not through any preaching we did, but through the ministry of the Word itself.

In Uganda, many students who have benefited from Bible studies in their schools have encouraged the formation of small cell groups in their churches. The benefits have spilled over into church life. Many of these same students have become leaders in the church, serving as elders and teachers.

Aggrey Mugisha, Uganda

# 2
# The Pilgrim's Purpose

---

*The only ultimate disaster that can befall us,*
*I have come to realize,*
*is to feel ourselves to be at home here on earth.*
*As long as we are aliens,*
*we cannot forget our true homeland.*
MALCOLM MUGGERIDGE

As PILGRIMS TRAVEL TO THEIR TRUE HOMELAND, SMALL GROUPS provide dynamic settings for progress in the journey. But what makes a good small group? Most people have fairly definite opinions about this—and there seldom is consensus among them!

Some might say, "Mrs. Smith's Sunday school class is the biggest waste of time. All they do is sit around in a circle and pool their ignorance." Or, "In Mr. Baker's class people stare at the back of other people's heads and endure a third-rate second sermon." But some people prefer Mr. Baker's lecture class because they don't have to think or talk—and they don't have to get too personal. It's much easier to sit and listen to an expert than to discuss problems in a marriage or tensions with rebellious teenagers.

Others don't say much about the kind of group they prefer, but they vote with their feet. They simply don't show up for Sunday school, or they attend the kind of group most in tune with their personalities. Some people won't attend a small group unless there's a published agenda and parliamentary procedure is closely followed. Others resist any obvious structure, preferring informal, "laid-back" settings.

## People vs. Task

Individuals seem to fall into two rather different group-personality styles. The *people-oriented* personality often prefers groups that have little structure, laissez-faire leadership, interpersonal "transparency," and openness in sharing. This kind of person feels that the purpose of the group is to build up individuals within the group. The *task-oriented* personality often prefers formal structure, directive leadership, advice from experts, and a pre-determined purpose. This kind of person prefers a specific agenda with no surprises. Often the task-oriented person would rather not be in a small group at all. He or she sees this setting as an inefficient means of communicating knowledge or accomplishing a task.

Some say it doesn't matter which group style is used as long as it is appropriate for the specific task at hand or for the maturity level of the group. Others attempt to solve the dilemma by encouraging groups to be strong both in their regard for people and their regard for the task.

So what is more important—the task or the person? Both the people-oriented and the task-oriented personalities can find examples to support their preferences from Scripture. Those favoring the task-orientation might emphasize the Great Commission (Matt. 28:18-20), while those favoring the people-orientation might emphasize the Great Commandment (Matt. 22:37-38). Scripture does not give detailed or direct answers about how small groups should be structured. We can't build a theory and practice of small groups by proof-texting isolated verses from the Bible.

**Questions to Ask**

To understand why groups work and how they work, we need to ask broader questions about the purpose of life and the nature of people. A model to help clarify the often-hidden assumptions about groups may be helpful.[1]

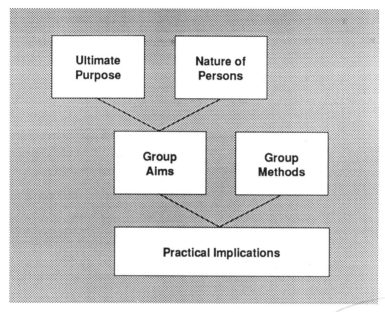

This model helps us to reflect on five questions:

1. What is the *ultimate purpose* of life? Too often people debate the purpose of groups without considering the ultimate questions of life.

2. What is the *nature of persons*? Are people basically lazy and ignorant, or are people basically good and trustworthy? What are the implications of Creation and the Fall? What is the nature of people who will make up our small groups?

3. What are the *aims of small groups*? An understanding of group aims needs to grow out of answers to the first two questions. Too often people decide the aims of a group on the basis of personality

style instead of a commitment to the ultimate purpose of life and an understanding of the nature of persons.

4. Which *methods* will be most likely to accomplish the aims of the group? Methods are often based on fads or reaction to fads without much consideration about how these will promote or hinder the aims of the group. Sometimes the use of innovative methods becomes the primary aim!

5. What are the practical, specific *implications* of our understanding about group methods and aims? If we believe certain things about the ultimate purpose of life, the nature of persons, group aims, and methods, what should these assumptions look like in actual practice?

It's healthy to reflect on each of these five questions, and it's also important to relate the five questions to each other. A group leader could have a fairly good understanding of each individual principle without having a consistent, unified theory. The five questions build on each other and reinforce each other.

### Bogged Down by Secondary Goals

The pilgrim metaphor provides a helpful focus for understanding groups since pilgrims have an ultimate purpose that goes beyond any narrow agenda.

In the '60s and '70s there was a lot of talk about the "human potential movement." Sensitivity groups, encounter groups, and growth groups made their way into church systems. "Unleashing human potential" became the goal of these groups. But the self-actualization of the pilgrim is not the ultimate purpose of a healthy group. Building an atmosphere of caring and openness is important, but that is not the final standard for measuring the success of a group. It's a means to a greater end.

In the church today, pilgrims often get bogged down with the near-sighted task of merely growing larger groups. Small groups are seen as the answer to church growth. Pastors look at the world's largest church in Korea, which is largely based on small cell groups, and long to experience that kind of growth. So some small groups are formed merely for the sake of numerical growth. Recruiting more pilgrims is a worthy activity, but not the ultimate purpose.

Neither size or quality is the ultimate purpose of a pilgrim group. One of the great temptations pilgrims face is substituting a good but less important goal for the ultimate purpose. Goals like growth and intimacy must be measured by a bigger standard. If there is no ultimate purpose, the less important purpose becomes an idol, and the true purpose is truncated.

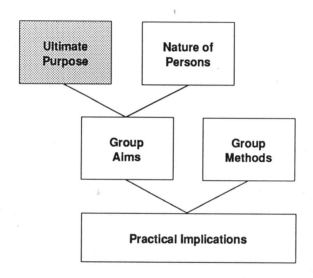

### The Ultimate Purpose

Deuteronomy 6:5 summarizes the ultimate purpose of life: "*Love the LORD your God with all your heart* and with all your soul and with all your strength." All our actions, whether eating or drinking or whatever we do, are to be done for the *glory of God*.[2] Paul considered everything else in life as loss compared to the surpassing greatness of *knowing Christ Jesus*.[3] We are commanded to wor-ship the LORD in the splendor of his holiness.[4] "Let everything that has breath *praise the LORD*."[5] All Scripture reminds and challenges us to love, glorify, know, worship, and praise the Lord. Nothing else in life has meaning without this ultimate purpose. Everything we do either helps us or hinders us in the quest of knowing God. The only final standard for evaluating the effectiveness of any activity or method is to determine whether it helps us to love God with more of our heart, soul, mind, and strength.

This ultimate purpose is the standard for measuring all other purposes. Whether the small group is a church building committee, an intimate discipleship group, or an adult Sunday school lecture, the ultimate purpose is the same.

Groups can grow in numbers, accomplish great tasks, and com-municate Bible knowledge yet still be worthless and even danger-ous if they don't contribute to the ultimate purpose of loving and glorifying God.

Different kinds of groups will have different group aims. But these aims must be evaluated by how they promote or hinder the ultimate purpose. Too often *aims* become ultimate purposes.

So not only is it important that we have the right ultimate purpose, but it is equally important that the ultimate purpose powerfully influences everything else in life. Most biblically based groups would agree that their ultimate purpose is to glorify God, but too often the purpose becomes lost in a file-folder somewhere and doesn't actually influence the details of group planning.

The ultimate purpose can be pictured as the core of an onion. The core—loving God, knowing God, praising God, and glorifying God—is the heart of the group. This core keeps all the other values in place. Group aims and methods will collapse if there is no foundational center. Too often groups get so involved with the details of group activities that the core slips out, and no one seems to notice.

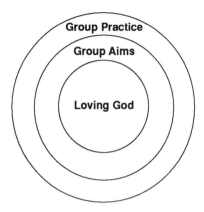

The driving force behind group aims and methods must be the burning desire to bring glory to God. Fellowship is a valuable means for accomplishing this ultimate purpose. But when fellowship becomes the end instead of the means, the group will make an idol out of itself. Bible study is also an excellent activity, but when it becomes the ultimate purpose, the group will degenerate into mere intellectual activity. Evangelism is a God-given task, but when evangelism becomes the ultimate purpose, the task will deteriorate into a numbers game.

Group methods and aims can vary depending on the personality style of people in the group. Groups are not good or bad depending on methods. People-oriented personalities may prefer more interpersonal sharing. Task-oriented personalities may prefer more structure. So what makes a good small group? The foundational criteria for evaluating a small group is whether or not it helps people to know and love God.

### Questions for Reflection
**1.** Think about the group experiences of which you have been a part. Did these groups have a sense of purpose? What was it?

**2.** Give examples you know of groups that were not guided by the ultimate purpose—growing in Christ and glorifying God. What did these groups see as their purpose?

**3.** If you are in a small group now, how is it contributing to your ultimate purpose for living? If it isn't, how could you help to clarify its purpose and bring it in line with your ultimate purpose?

### Notes
**1.** Adapted from a model by William K. Frankena, *Philosophy of Education* (New York: The MacMillan Company, 1965), pp. 4-10.
**2.** 1 Corinthians 10:31.
**3.** Philippians 3:8,10.
**4.** 1 Chronicles 16:29.
**5.** Psalm 150:6.

### Why Small Groups Are Important to Me

I have always known that the Bible was the most important book our family owned. It was read and quoted, memorized, and carried to Sunday school, where both my parents taught. Back then I would have told you the Bible is the powerful Word of God—but that was secondhand information. Today if you asked me, I would affirm its power with conviction based on abundant evidence.

I gathered most of the evidence in small group studies. My first exposure came during my freshman year in college. A few of us met in the dorm to examine the gospel of Mark. Armed with good questions in a studyguide, we discovered answers. The Bible became understandable. We who were from different backgrounds learned to listen to each other. Our diversity sharpened the discussion, pushing us back to the text to check our answers. I realized that I didn't need to defend the Bible, but just carefully examine it. Truth speaks for itself.

The small group increased my understanding of the passage. By myself, I had a few ideas of its meaning and application. But others widened my insights and enriched me. The group had a self-correcting effect on a personal distortion.

Later, while teaching school, I joined a group of Christian peers for a weekly support and study group. We prayed each other through first job traumas and struggles to apply biblical principles in every area of our lives. At every stage in my life and in every location, I've been in a small study group. I can't stand not to be. I've seen God change me and my friends as we take steps of faith and obedience together.

Martha Reapsome, Illinois

# 3
# The Nature of Pilgrims

*We should not think of our fellowship*
*with other Christians as a spiritual luxury . . .*
*We should recognize rather that such fellowship*
*is a spiritual necessity; for God has made us*
*in such a way that our fellowship with Himself*
*is fed by our fellowship with fellow Christians . . .*
J.I. PACKER

P ILGRIMS AREN'T PERFECT—AT LEAST NOT YET. BUT THEY HAVE GREAT
dignity and worth, even when stuck in the Slough of Despond or
chained in Doubting Castle. Though pilgrims are created in the
image of God, they are still "prone to wander." An understanding
of the nature of pilgrims is vital to a theory of small groups.

## The Dilemma

Our assumptions about group members are often hidden or below
the level of our awareness.

If people are "basically good," one kind of group theory is
appropriate. But if people are "intrinsically evil," another theory is
suitable. And what if both of these descriptions are true? In fact,
this is the dilemma: people have two basic realities about them.
They are created in the image of God, and they are also fallen. Both

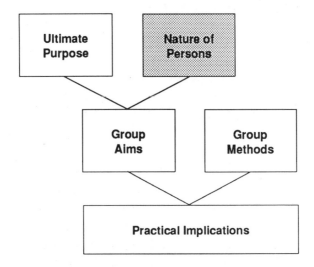

Creation and the Fall have tremendous implications for understanding small groups.

The first three chapters of Genesis summarize the primary dilemma. Genesis 1 and 2 describe the creation of the world and of men and women. God created Adam and Eve in his own image and saw that his creation was very good. Yet Adam and Eve sinned by disobeying God and were forced to live under a curse, banished from the Garden of Eden (Gen. 3). God's image in people was marred by the Fall. So people became capable of great rebellion against God. As people continued to turn away from God, their "thinking became futile, hearts were darkened, and they became fools." As a result, God gave them over to a depraved mind (Rom. 1:21-22, 28). Since the Fall, human beings have not been what God intended them to be.

Because people are created in the image of God and also fallen, any theory of groups must take into account both aspects. One without the other will lead to heresy and cause harm. Yet the two seem to contradict each other. How can a theory of groups grow out of two necessary but contradictory principles? Should we treat people like gods or like machines? How can we do both? Group aims, group methods, and group practice must take this dilemma into account.

Think how wonderful it would be if each person in a group was always loving, kind, and hard-working. What if no one person tried to dominate or manipulate the group? What if leaders always looked out for the good of the group and had no selfish ambition? What if there never was any conflict? Harmonious, loving, hard-working groups would be the norm if people were not affected by the Fall.

Those who neglect the teaching of the Fall build a dangerous theory of groups. Recent trends in psychology emphasize the goodness of persons,[1] and New Age teaching assumes that people are gods. Self-actualization, freedom, and openness are important goals for such groups. Small group leaders facilitate inner reflection and sharing. The assumption is that if people will only let their inner selves grow, the result will be goodness, love, and harmony. Such assumptions ignore the inherent sinfulness of people. If the *nature of persons* is assumed to be inherently good, then the *ultimate purpose* becomes the task of liberating that inner goodness. But making a god of people is idolatry.

On the other hand, those who neglect the fact that people are created in the image of God also construct a dangerous theory of groups. What if people were not created in the image of God? What if sinfulness, greed, and self-love were the whole nature of persons? There would be no reason to assume that people have internal moral standards and potential for growth. People would simply become conditioned animals or machines with no freedom or dignity.[2]

## Implications for Groups

Understanding the nature of persons has compelling implications for small groups. If leaders assume that people can't be trusted, they feel the need to control the group tightly with rewards and punishments. The inner development of the person is replaced by the training of outward behavior. Group members cannot be trusted to know what they need to learn, nor can they be trusted to use inner resources to solve problems for themselves. (Often such leaders feel they are less influenced by the Fall than others in the group!)

From this unsound perspective, small groups in a church need to be closely supervised with a controlled curriculum. Since there is little respect for the insights and experiences of group members, a lecture by an "expert" is considered more appropriate than "pooling ignorance." The doctrine of the priesthood of all believers has little significance for such small group theory. It assumes that the average person is not capable of correctly understanding or applying Scripture, so the pastor or some other authority figure needs to decide on rules of behavior that people in the church should follow. Small groups are used to hold people accountable for obeying the rules.

And what about those who neglect the implications of the Fall? Such leaders focus on the inherent goodness of human beings, naively assuming that goodness will express itself if given the right conditions. Leaders working under this assumption hesitate to give guidance and direction because freedom and self-actualization are such important goals. The power of sin is ignored, and content is downplayed for the sake of interaction and personal relevance. The emphasis is on "getting in touch with one's feelings." So groups flounder without the foundational content of the Word of God. Leaders fail to give direction for fear of squelching freedom and human potential.

So this is the dilemma for building a theory of small groups: people are created in the image of God, yet fallen. Both facts are true, even though the two seem incompatible in group theory. However, one without the other leads to dangerous group practice. People are neither gods nor mere animals, yet they have qualities of both.

Redemption is God's process for making bad people into good people. The bad news is that we are sinners. The Good News is that Christ died to take away our sins. He rose again and sits at the right hand of the Father to help us become like him. And he's coming again to make us perfect. Our ultimate purpose is to love the Lord with all our heart, soul, mind, and strength. Our nature is that we are fallen and selfish, yet we have the potential to be like Christ. If both statements are true, then the most important aim of the small group is to foster our development as individuals until we "become mature, attaining to the whole measure of the fullness of Christ" (Eph. 4:13).

Development toward Christlikeness is a necessary step toward reaching the ultimate purpose of loving God more fully. So promoting human development as designed by God is the most important aim for groups.

### The Nature of Human Development

The Bible gives the only absolute and authoritative teaching about the nature of persons, but important insights can also be gained through social science research on human development. God's truth in his Word will never contradict his truth in his world. As we understand the way people grow and develop, we can structure groups to promote that growth.

### The Stages of Development

The work of Swiss psychologist Jean Piaget gives valuable insights into the nature of human development. His findings can help to develop a theory of small groups. Piaget is best known for exploring the stages of mental development from birth to adulthood.[3]

According to Piaget, the process of growth is like the widening ripples caused by a stone falling into a pond. Each stage of human development leads to wider horizons and broader perspectives.

The more developed person can appreciate a point of view from a greater number of perspectives. And perspectivism is essential to healthy small groups. As people grow in perspectivism, they can "rejoice with those who rejoice and weep with those who weep." Perspectivism makes discussion possible as people listen and interact with each other's views.

Parents know that small children are egocentric. They can see the world only from their own limited perspective. A wise parent knows it does no good to tell a hungry baby to wait sixty seconds for milk. God didn't create screaming babies with the mental capacity to contemplate the future.

As children grow older, their awareness of the points of view of other people increases, but the depth of their interaction with others is rather shallow. This is why young children tend to interact in what is called "parallel play." They are aware of other children playing near them, but they "play alone together."[4] Minimal small-group interaction for children begins to take place about the age of seven. They can now discuss concrete situations with each other and begin to take the perspective of other children. But they are still not able to discuss abstract concepts such as "sharing." For the seven-year-old, sharing means letting another person use one particular object. So a child may remember to share an umbrella but not a jump rope. Sharing in the abstract is a difficult concept for children.

From about the age of twelve, plus or minus a few years, perspectivism and interaction grow rapidly. Teenagers are able to see themselves as others see them. Such perspectivism is a strong motivation for boys to begin combing their hair and for girls to pay special attention to what they wear. Teens are growing in their ability to participate in small-group discussions because they are better able to analyze and reflect on comments from others in the group. Genuine dialogue in small groups is now possible.

Most adults are capable of genuine dialogue, but some adults don't have a lot of experience in "wrestling" with new ideas from different perspectives. Even in adult groups, discussion is often a string of unrelated comments from different members of the group. Genuine interaction with the ideas of other adults is not something to be taken for granted. The developmental level of adults will profoundly affect the dynamics of a group.

## Promoting Development

Piaget has generated important studies on the factors that *promote* development. Two important factors are *social interaction* and the process of *exploring tensions*, or "disequilibration." People tend to grow and develop as they *struggle with problems in groups.*[5]

Interestingly, people tend to make the most progress in their thinking when things don't make sense! For example, little Billy, a small child, may have a single mental category for animals—his family's dog, Fido. Everything with four legs, a tail, and a wet nose is a dog. When Billy sees Scratch, the neighbor's calico cat with four legs, a kind of tail, and a sort of wet nose, Billy calls Scratch a dog. The process continues until Billy sees a cow, or any animal that doesn't fit the "dog" category. The cow has some of the characteristics of a dog, yet is very different. The cow doesn't fit with Fido and Scratch in the child's mental category. This causes "disequilibration." The problem prompts the child to construct a broader mental category for animals and produces cognitive development.

Adults also grow as they explore tensions and create new categories. This process is enhanced through interaction with other adults. This means that small groups can provide an ideal setting for healthy growth! For example, when a Presbyterian and a Pentecostal think together over a passage in the Book of Acts, it's very possible that healthy "disequilibration" will take place. As they explore the tensions of their differences in interpretation, both will see things they never saw before in that passage. Interaction with people who have different perspectives can be a powerful stimulus to growth. We'll look at more implications for this in another chapter.

Ultimately, growth toward Christlikeness is a gift of God. Each Christian in a group has spiritual gifts, so the group itself can become a means of grace. Though groups can facilitate growth, godly development is a result of God's grace (1 Cor. 3:6-7).

Insights about the ultimate purpose of life and the nature of persons can suggest specific aims for small groups. In the next chapter we'll look at what these specific aims might look like.

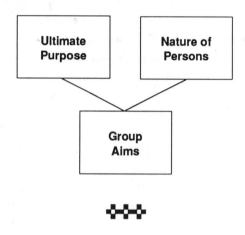

**Questions for Reflection**

**1.** What implications do Creation and the Fall have for understanding the nature of persons?

**2.** What might these implications mean for small group practice?

**3.** As you observe groups of different ages, notice their differing abilities in perspective-taking.

**4.** If growth takes place through social interaction and through exploring tensions, how can small groups be effective promoters of growth?

## Notes

1. This emphasis can be seen in the work of Carl R. Rogers. See "Toward Becoming a Fully Functioning Person" in *Perceiving, Behaving Becoming* (Washington, D.C.: Association for Supervision and Curriculum Development, NEA, 1962). Rogers is often right in what he does say, but wrong in what he doesn't say.

2. This is the view of B.F. Skinner as described in his book *Beyond Freedom and Dignity* (New York: Bantam, 1971).

3. A good introduction to some of Piaget's major ideas is *Piaget's Theory of Cognitive Development* by Barry J. Wadsworth (New York: David McKay Co., Inc., 1974). See also Jean Piaget and Barbel Inhelder, *The Psychology of the Child* (New York: Basic Books, Inc., 1969).

4. The development of perspective-taking in children is discussed by Robert Selman, "The Development of Socio-Cognitive Understanding: A Guide to Educational and Clinical Practice" in *Morality: Theory, Research and Social Issues*, ed. Thomas Lickona (New York: Holt, Rinehart and Winston, 1976).

5. *Piaget's Theory of Cognitive Development*, p. 30.

## *Why Small Groups Are Important to Me*

Wednesday evening. The coffee percolator is making contented burps and gurgles. At 7:28 the first person arrives, helps herself to coffee or fresh-brewed tea. The room fills with 10-15 people by 7:40. Conversations buzz; people sip. I clear my throat. "Let's turn to Luke 14 . . ." It's time to shift gears, settle into the Word, feed ourselves.

Our small group is a lively oasis; a time for hearing God by hearing friends discuss what his Word says, means. From the hot blast of work, pain, loneliness, hassles, joy, and achievement we enter each other's shade and drink God's draft. We cheer each other's triumphs; bear each other's burdens. The bond thus forged is strength for the road ahead and salve for the wounds collected since we last met.

Ninety minutes later we say good-bye. Some hugs are exchanged; a few plan to meet for Saturday breakfast; three will do contact evangelism at the mall on Friday and two couples are going to orchestra tomorrow night. They go off into the night and a satisfied hush descends on the room.

Larry Sibley, Pennsylvania

# 4

# Aims for
# Pilgrim Groups

*Our Father refreshes us on the journey
with some pleasant inns, but will not encourage us
to mistake them for home.*
C.S. LEWIS

WHEN PILGRIMS MEET TOGETHER, THERE IS A SENSE OF JOY AND excitement. They tell each other about an encouraging encounter, describe a magnificent sunset, or give suggestions for using the Map. But pilgrims also know the need for comfort and guidance. They meet to bind wounds and warn each other of dangers along the road. They challenge each other to point others to the path and to become involved in the sufferings of those who have not yet set their hearts on pilgrimage. They know the purpose of their journey and that purpose gives focus to their more specific group aims. Pilgrim groups know they must not lose sight of the ultimate purpose—loving and praising the King. And though they affirm that pilgrims are created in the image of God, they also recognize that pilgrims are inclined to get lost and wounded. Aims for pilgrim groups grow naturally out of a compelling commitment to the *ultimate purpose* of pilgrims and a solid understanding of the *nature of pilgrims.*

**The Need for Foundations**

When pilgrim groups disregard the ultimate purpose, their group aims lack focus. Sometimes pilgrims get so involved with a *task* that they forget the ultimate goal. For example, members of a church committee might get so absorbed with building a beautiful church that they wound pilgrims in the process. When a task becomes the ultimate purpose, pilgrims will be hurt rather than helped.

Sometimes "management experts" make efficiency the ultimate purpose. They say that good management is "using pilgrims to accomplish the task," and the ultimate purpose becomes the efficient use of pilgrims. We need to use the task to develop pilgrims, not pilgrims to accomplish the task. Developing pilgrims *is* the task! Task-oriented committees need to make sure that their task contributes to the ultimate purpose. Even such important tasks as evangelism, church growth, discipleship, or social action can be detrimental if divorced from the ultimate purpose. God has given pilgrims vital tasks, but these must contribute to the primary goal of helping pilgrims to love their King more fully.

Pilgrims desperately need loving, caring *relationships* in order to survive the perils of the road. Loving other pilgrims is an important way to show love for the King. But groups can err in being so relationship-oriented that the quality of the relationship becomes the goal. Relationships have a greater purpose. A pilgrim group becomes pathological if pilgrims merely sit in a circle singing about the blessed tie that binds them together. Pilgrim fellowship must be active and goal-oriented. Pilgrims need to care deeply about those who don't follow the King.

Pilgrims also need to *study the Map*—the Word of God. But even Map-study can become an end in itself. Pilgrims might study what other scholars have said about the Map, translate the Map from the original languages, and study the history of Map-making—yet never make progress toward their destination! It's important for scholars to study the Map of the Word and even to spend their whole lives doing so, but they must always remember the *purpose* of maps. Maps are meant to help travelers reach a destination. Small groups need to study the Bible, with the aim of helping pilgrims make progress toward the goal.

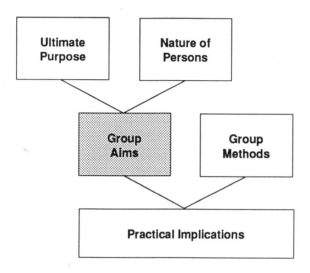

## Group Aims

Pilgrims don't need to wait until they reach the Celestial City before they can love and know God. The most important *group aim* is to help pilgrims fulfill their ultimate purpose. The more pilgrims become like Christ, the more fully they will know, love, and praise God. Nurturing groups can help pilgrims in that process. So every small group will have aims for its individual members and aims for the group as a whole.

Often there is tension between the individual and the group. Individualists do not want to yield their personal autonomy to the control of a group. In the book *Habits of the Heart*, Robert Bellah writes,

Individualism lies at the very core of American culture. . . . We believe in the dignity, indeed the sacredness, of the individual. Anything that would violate our right to think for ourselves, judge for ourselves, make our own decisions, live our lives as we see fit, is not only morally wrong, it is sacrilegious.[1]

Yet for Jesus' followers, community is not optional. It is normative. We are members of the "household of God" (1 Tim. 3:15). This doesn't mean groups have the right to squelch personal freedom in a cult-like manner. It does mean that individual pilgrims must put kingdom goals ahead of the self-seeking aspirations of the American Dream. Groups need to nurture individual pilgrims and also build a healthy community. But seen in the bigger framework, neither the individual nor the group is the ultimate focus. The glory of God is the ultimate purpose.

**Individual Goals**

Before pilgrims can mature, they must be born!—born again into the family of God. Then they are ready for the journey toward maturity in Christ.

As pilgrims grow in holiness, they begin to overcome the effects of the Fall, and they give glory to God more fully. The standard for perfection is Christ himself. One of the best descriptions of Christlikeness is the fruit of the Spirit: "love, joy, peace, patience, kindness, goodness, faithfulness, gentleness and self-control." The passage continues, "Those who belong to Christ have crucified the sinful nature with its passions and desires. Since we live by the Spirit let us keep in step with the Spirit" (Gal. 5:22-26). These are important guidelines for pilgrims. Pilgrims become more and more like Christ as they crucify the sinful nature and evidence the work of the Spirit in their journey.

There is a defensive aspect to the pilgrimage. Pilgrims must be equipped to defend themselves against the darts of the Evil One by putting on the whole armor of God. But pilgrims can also go on the offensive. Much of the land through which pilgrims travel is temporarily under the control of the enemy. This means that pilgrims are "working behind enemy lines" when they try to convince other pilgrims to join them. Pilgrim groups are like commando units, doing as much harm to the enemy as possible until the land is reclaimed by the coming King.

Pilgrims won't be fully like Christ until he appears and they see him as he is (1 John 3:2). But holiness is a progressive goal.

## Group Activities

The purpose of a small group is to help pilgrims in their goal of becoming more like Christ. To do this, pilgrims need to love each other, study the Map, talk to the King, and point other pilgrims to the path. There are other important aims, but these four are among the most important.

A wheel won't work unless it is completely rounded. Groups need to aim at a balance of activities. Without love for each other, pilgrims cannot survive the journey. Without Bible study, they easily take the wrong path and become discouraged. Without prayer, pilgrims lose out on the supernatural assistance they need. Without evangelism, pilgrims become self-centered, and thwart the King's plan. Groups that focus on only one, two, or three of the aims will eventually get into trouble.

## Love Each Other

Jesus said that all the commandments could be summarized in two: "Love the Lord your God with all your heart, with all your soul, and with all your mind.... Love your neighbor as yourself" (Matt. 22:37, 39). The two are inextricably bound together, reflecting our ultimate purpose and our group aim.

Small groups are ideal settings for practicing and demonstrating love. This is one of the unique ways that small groups complement the activities of larger groups. Indeed, love was the distinguishing mark of the early church groups that gathered in homes. It caused the pagans of that day to marvel, "see how they love one another!" Members of pilgrim groups don't wear uniforms or special pins. They don't have distinguishing hairstyles like Hare Krishna cultists or special handshakes like members of some clubs. Their distinguishing characteristic is love.

Some designate this particular group function as "fellowship." But this kind of love is more than the coffee-and-doughnuts activity that most people think of as fellowship. This is not just "any kind of love." It is Jesus' love, demonstrated on the cross, and it permeates every aspect of the group. Love motivates group members to prod each other on toward obedience to the Scriptures they study together. Love prompts group members to rejoice together in joy and weep together in sorrow. It encourages genuine prayer as pilgrims bear each other's burdens. And it's love that compels group members to reach out to lost and wounded pilgrims. Love is central to the goals and activities of every group.

A group may have the best Bible study leaders, be well organized, self-sacrificing, and even give all its money to the poor, but if group members don't have love, they are merely a resounding gong or a clanging cymbal (1 Cor. 13:1). All small groups—whether the church board, the finance committee, an adult Sunday school class, or a home discipleship group—must make love for one another the highest priority. No matter how much is accomplished in other areas, the group will do more harm than good without this kind of love.

## Study the Bible

The Bible is the map, the guide book, and the authoritative blueprint for all pilgrim activities. It is the primary source of encouragement for discouraged pilgrims and the only diagram for pointing other pilgrims to the King. It gives the purpose for living and is our source of hope in the next world.

> Our first spiritual discipline for knowing God is Bible study. How else can we escape the limits of our culture's majority view, the limits of our own reason, the limits even of our own Christian fellowship? All of these may be warped by human ignorance and selfishness. We need a guide independent of our culture and our reason. Fortunately, God has given us such a guide in his Word. We must be like the Bereans whom Paul praised because they "examined the Scriptures every day to see if what Paul said was true" (Acts 17:11). And as we take the Bible on our laps, it is an awesome thing to realize that thousands of Russians and Africans and Chinese and Nicaraguans are doing the same thing. We meet together as equals around the Word of God. Together we probe our reference group, our heritage, our roots.[2]

Not all groups meet primarily for the purpose of Bible study, but the Bible should guide every meeting. Church board meetings often begin with an obligatory devotional that no one pays attention to while waiting to get to the "hot" items on the agenda. The Bible should remind committees of the ultimate purpose of the church and should be referred to many times during the meeting as people seek wisdom on specific issues. Other groups spend most of their time sharing needs and praying for each other. Some of these groups see Bible study as a mental academic activity that takes up valuable time which could better be used for getting to "real needs." But Bible study should guide prayer requests and be used to encourage weary pilgrims. Using Scripture as a basis for prayer is a powerful way to intercede.[3] While Bible study doesn't need to be the dominant focus of every group, it does need to be a part of every small group.

**Talk to God**

Small groups are workshops for prayer—labs where we can experiment and learn the life of prayer. Each pilgrim needs to be prayed for personally. "In everything, by prayer and petition, with thanksgiving, present your requests to God" (Phil. 4:6). Pilgrims are not expected to fight the enemy alone—they can't. Powerful help is available from the Lord of the universe—but in God's plan, they must request his help.

Thanksgiving is also commanded. The life of the pilgrim is filled not only with dangers and difficulties, but with blessings and answers to prayer. Pilgrims need to thank the King for times of refreshment and even for small victories.

Prayer and praise need to be part of every small group agenda. Pilgrims realize that God expects them to do difficult things when they obey his Word. Through prayer, the Holy Spirit gives them supernatural abilities to obey Scripture. Scripture needs prayer and prayer needs Scripture. Pilgrims facing the enemy must "pray in the Spirit on all occasions, with all kinds of prayers and requests" (Eph. 6:18).

Bob and Win Couchman describe the need for small group prayer like this:

Wouldn't it be terrible if all we had to offer each other for our great needs were wishes? Imagine that you are at your regular group meeting and everything is as it has always been except that there is no such thing as prayer.

Dick: "I have something to share with everybody. I lost my job today. My boss walked into my office after lunch and informed me that my whole engineering group is out."

Hans: "I can't believe what you're saying. Didn't you just get an excellent report from him about your performance?"

Dick: "Unfortunately, that has nothing to do with it. Because of the economic situation, somebody higher up decided that the number of groups has to be cut and for several reasons that have nothing to do with me, ours was the group that got it."

Judy: "I'm thinking right away about your family. We've got to do something. Let me think. . . ."

Hans: "It isn't much, Dick, but I do offer you my sincerest sympathy and best wishes. I'll keep my ears open."

Judy: "My best wishes, too, Dick. I wish there were something more I could do. This is so frustrating."

Others in the group: "We're really sorry, Dick." "Good luck, Dick." "We'll really be thinking about you." "Keep in touch, brother."

A wish is a pebble thrown by a child. A prayer is a rocket launched. In faith, God's child prays in the name of Jesus. The Spirit directs the prayer in accordance with God's will and, in accordance with that will, God acts.

Our wishes cannot produce results. Our prayers? Listen: "By means of his power working in us [he] is able to do so much more than we can ever ask for, or even think of: to God be the glory in the church and in Christ Jesus for all time for ever and ever! Amen" (Eph. 3:20-21, TEV).[4]

## Point Others to Christ

Not every small group needs to be directly evangelistic, but every small group must be concerned about lost pilgrims and demonstrate that concern in some way. The normal tendency for groups is to become inward looking, to be concerned about each other, and to ignore the task God has given. Evangelism needs to grow out of genuine love for lost pilgrims, out of a desire to serve the King, and out of the need to use this important task to develop pilgrims.

Small groups of all sorts can show concern for the lost. Church committees should give high priority to budget funds and time for missions and evangelism. Sunday school classes need activities that encourage the involvement of class members in evangelism. Small groups need to pray for members who have opportunities to witness in their jobs or neighborhoods. And they need to pray as a group for world outreach.[5]

Service and outreach will strengthen each member's personal walk with God. It will also give new vitality and balance to the group. And most important, it will contribute to the spread of God's kingdom in the world.

This outward focus won't detract from the unity of the group—it will enhance it. Small groups can demonstrate God's love by the way they care for each other. They can also mediate God's love by carrying "the ministry of reconciliation" (2 Cor. 5:18) to those around them. And they can have a powerful worldwide outreach through prayer.

## In Summary

The primary purpose of all small groups is to help pilgrims become like Christ as they evidence the fruit of the Spirit and other biblical character traits. All small groups should have a primary emphasis on demonstrating God's love and should include Bible study, prayer, and evangelism. These aims should be seen in all groups— administrative committees, evangelistic training groups, Bible study groups, or fellowship and prayer groups. Such groups will help fulfill the ultimate purpose of loving God and will build on a biblical philosophy of the nature of persons.

### Questions for Reflection

**1.** How is group prayer and group Bible study different from individual prayer and study?

**2.** Have you experienced any tensions between personal goals and group goals? If so, how did you resolve the tension?

**3.** Think about the health of your small group. Does it include the four aims that characterize a healthy group? If not, what can you do to encourage a healthy balance?

### Notes

**1.** Robert N. Bellah, Richard Madsen, William M. Sullivan, Ann Swidler, and Steven M. Tipton, *Habits of the Heart: Individualism and Commitment in American Life* (New York: Harper and Row, 1985), p. 142.

**2.** Miriam Adeney, *A Time for Risking* (Portland, Oreg.: Multnomah Press, 1987), p. 97.

**3.** A helpful guide for using the Scriptures in prayer is *Pocket Prayers* by Robert C. Savage (Wheaton, Ill.: Tyndale, 1982).

**4.** Bob & Win Couchman, *Small Groups: Timber to Build Up God's House* (Wheaton, Ill.: Shaw Publishers, 1982), pp. 57-58.

**5.** A helpful resource to help your group pray for worldwide outreach is *Operation World* by Patrick Johnstone (William Carey Library, P.O. Box 128-C, Pasadena, CA 91104). It outlines specific needs in every country with suggestions for prayer.

### Why Small Groups Are Important to Me

It I were asked, "What was the one thing that most helped you 'bond' with the people on your mission field?" I would not hesitate to answer, "small group Bible studies." It was through my own participation in one that I gradually came to understand how my new Kenyan friends perceived their problems, what they felt to be their blessings, and how I could best pray for them. And I am convinced that unless one is unusually skilled at interpersonal relationships, involvement in a small group is one of the fastest ways to get "inside" another culture.

Like many other small groups, ours began as a simple Monday night Bible study in our compound of eighteen maisonettes or townhouses. Because it is dangerous and difficult to go out at night by bus in Nairobi, most churches have no mid-week service. We found that the most convenient method of grouping was for Christians of several denominations to gather together within walking distance of our homes, where we could literally hear any crying babies that awoke.

There were other advantages: those who were shy could remain silent until they felt sure of themselves. Those who were put off by a church did not feel intimidated by a home. The seats were definitely more comfortable than the benches at church! No refreshments were served; the a cappella singing was refreshment to the soul.

There was one special plus in our polyglot metropolis: it didn't matter that we all spoke some English and some Swahili; we could pray in our mother tongues during the prayer time, and no one minded.

Of course, we had some discouragements, too. We had one domineering member who insisted on correcting others' mistakes, even to the point of having the entire group sing over again five verses of a chorus because we had missed the pitch on several notes. (You could see the hurt in the faces of those she silenced with her quick tongue.)

Other difficulties for me personally, and I'm sure for others, were the lateness of the hour (many and mighty were the yawns I suppressed) and the shallowness of the study. Mixing new Christians with more mature Christians always makes it hard to match levels of interest. But generally speaking, it is mutually beneficial in other ways that make such a mix worth trying.

For us in Nairobi, small group Bible studies are the best way to fellowship with our Christian neighbors and have a strong testimony to those homes nearby who hear us singing and see us walking in and out with our Bibles and smiles. It has also been the biggest blessing in my life as an "outsider," a foreigner, helping me to feel loved and welcomed and understood in my own small group and helping me to love and understand the nationals.

Susan Bergman DeVries, Kenya

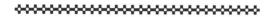

# 5
## Methods for Pilgrim Groups

*Faith is, in the end, a kind of homesickness—*
*for a home we have never visited*
*but have never once stopped longing for.*
PHILIP YANCEY

THE PROFESSOR FINALLY LOOKED UP FROM HIS LECTURE NOTES. "Pilgrims, pay attention! You must learn these facts if you want to get a diploma. The knowledge might help you to find the right path, but if not, at least you'll be certified as a Master Pilgrim." Week after week the lecturer droned on. Soon even the professor's best students found an excuse to drop out.

A small group of rebel pilgrims got so fed up with the professor that they formed their own small group. They made a rule that no one could teach information. They sat in a circle on the floor and shared the joys and sorrows of past or recent journeys. But the rebel group also became frustrated. The sharing method made them feel better, but it didn't help them find the right path, nor did it give them strength to climb difficult hills. Sharing problems was not enough. Soon pilgrims found "previous commitments" as an excuse to drop out of this group, too.

Methods that expound mere knowledge are deadly to small groups because they are divorced from the needs of life. Lecture by itself is not an adequate small group method. On the other hand, methods that merely encourage the sharing of life-needs without teaching knowledge will quickly prove irrelevant to pilgrims. And discussion by itself is not an adequate method for small groups either.

The greatest expert may be teaching the most valuable information in the world, but if the group doesn't know the importance of the information, the group disintegrates. Methods for small groups must help pilgrims blend their problems with authoritative answers from God's Word. Good methods integrate life and truth.

Some people love any new method that comes along. They devour the latest "ten easy methods for having a super-duper small group." "Don't give me all this theoretical baloney," they say. "Just tell me how to do it! Let the scholars worry about the philosophy. What I need to know is how I'm going to fill the next hour and a half. Let's get practical!" They jump from one methodological fad to another. One week their small group passively watches a video of an expert preacher. Another week they pounce to a computer-generated Bible study or a "primal scream" experience. A month later they get excited about a "spill-your-guts-in-front-of-perfect-strangers" method.

The other extreme is even more common. Small groups tend to get into a rut. Unreflective leaders get used to one method and exclaim, "We've always done it this way!" They ignore innovative methods, feeling that as long as they are teaching the truth, methods don't matter.

## Good Methods Tie Practice to Theory

There is nothing as practical as good theory, and good methods reflect good theory. Methods for small groups need to accomplish the *aims* of the group, build on a biblical understanding of the *nature of persons,* and contribute to the *ultimate purpose* of life. Healthy small groups use sound methods.

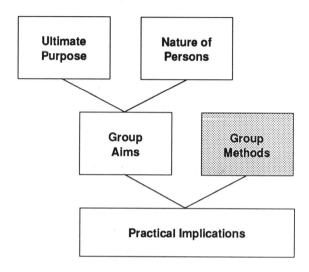

We often disagree more about methods than about content. For example, most parents are interested in the topic "How to Raise Children." But some parents want to learn about this through a video lecture given by an expert. Others want an inductive Bible study on parenting. Still others prefer to share how they were parented. Those interested in sharing might resist watching a video, and those interested in the video might detest personal sharing. The inductive Bible study folks might look down on the other two groups as a bit frivolous. Method is much more important than we imagine.

Many churches have adult Sunday morning electives. There are usually three kinds of classes. One might be a class on "The Christian and Money" given by a Christian financial planner. Another could be a lecture on the Book of Romans led by a college professor. A third class gets coffee and doughnuts and focuses on personal needs and prayer. The method used in each class tends to dictate the aim, rather than the aim guiding the method.

What makes for good methods in small groups? Is the best method the one that promotes the most personal relevance? Or the one that teaches the most authoritative content? Or one that promotes the most social interaction? Good methods involve more than personal preferences—they must foster the ultimate purpose and take into account the nature of persons.

### Good Methods Tie Life to Truth

The pilgrim metaphor helps to define group methods. Pilgrims need methods that are personally relevant—methods that will help them on their journey. But what is relevant? Knowledge of an authoritative map is extremely practical! Pilgrims also learn from other pilgrims. It makes sense, then, to intertwine personal relevance, authoritative content, and social interaction.

There are three sources of knowledge for pilgrims: the authoritative Map, their personal experiences, and the insights of other pilgrims. Good small group methods must use all three kinds of knowledge—not separately, but blended. The three sources of knowledge can be seen as rails in a fence, and good methods are like fence posts, tying the rails together.[1] All three kinds of learning are necessary, and good group methods need to incorporate all three.

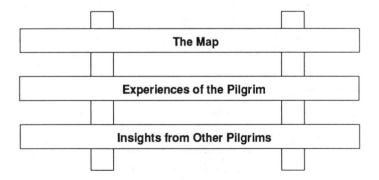

The Map

Experiences of the Pilgrim

Insights from Other Pilgrims

It doesn't make sense for pilgrims only to share personal experiences while ignoring the divine Map or disregarding the insights of other pilgrims. Nor do pilgrims study maps in isolation from their problems on the road. They have one eye on the Map and the other on the road. Methods for pilgrim groups need to focus on the Map and on the experiences of the pilgrim. Good methods will also include the insights and experiences of other pilgrims. A method that ignores even one of the rails is inadequate, and methods that highlight all three aspects but don't tie them together are also ineffective.

While the Bible is the only final authority for the Christian, the Holy Spirit works through all three rails. He works through the Word of God,[2] lives in each believer,[3] and gives gifts to all who belong to Christ.[4] Good methods for small groups use all the resources of the Holy Spirit—relating the experiences of life with the authority of Scripture in interaction with other Christians.

| M | The Bible | M |
|---|---|---|
| E | | E |
| T | Personal Experience | T |
| H | | H |
| O | Other Christians | O |
| D | | D |

Many small group methods emphasize only one of the three rails. Personal relevance methods accentuate the middle rail, social interaction methods highlight the bottom rail, and methods that teach information concentrate on the top rail. The best methods will include all three rails and will tie them together.

Many educators feel that there is an automatic link between biblical truth and the experiences of life. But the connection is not

automatic. Merely knowing Bible content is no guarantee that the
person will know how to apply it. Group methods must intentionally tie experience to the Bible. The connection between individual
experience and insights from other people is not automatic either.
It is quite possible for a person to be in a small group without
listening to the ideas of others in the group and without the
opportunity to get to know others in the group. Social interaction
must be built intentionally into the small group method.

While different kinds of groups may place different emphases
on each of the rails, all good methods for small groups should
include biblical content, personal experience, and group interaction. Hundreds of methods can be used to tie these three elements
together in small groups.

While good methods can intertwine the three rails in almost any
order, it is often useful to follow three steps. Begin with group
reflection on a life situation that is related to the Bible passage; then
study the Bible, and finally, ponder together how the Bible can
more fully control life experiences.

**Begin with Life**

It is usually best to begin Bible study with the needs and experiences of life. Some people argue that not all of the Bible is always
relevant to our present needs. But the Bible claims to be God-
breathed and useful—all of it (2 Tim. 3:16). All of Scripture is useful
for teaching, rebuking, correcting, and training in righteousness.
This is not to say that the Bible is true *only* if it is useful (that is the
error of pragmatism). But since Scripture is given to us by God, it
is useful. Each chapter of the Bible provides the stimulus for
teaching, rebuking, correcting, or training in righteousness. So it is
possible to teach through whole books of the Bible and still begin
each study with the life-needs of group members. The main task in
designing small group methods is to discover the link between
what God is telling us and the needs in our lives.

Another reason to begin with life-needs rather than content is that this is how Jesus most often began his teaching. He began with questions and then moved to answers. Jesus didn't immediately tell Nicodemus how to be born again but aroused his curiosity and stimulated him to ask leading questions. He started right where Nicodemus was, helping him to relate new truth to what he already knew.[5] Neither did Jesus tell the woman at the well that he was the Messiah until he actively involved her in thinking about physical water, living water, and true worship.[6] Jesus didn't teach the parable of the Good Samaritan until an expert in the law asked questions about how to inherit eternal life and tried to wiggle out of obeying the command to love his neighbor.[7] Even when Jesus initiated a discussion, he often began with a comment that perplexed his disciples and then followed up with a series of questions rather than answers.[8] Small groups today commonly begin with a study of a Bible passage and conclude, if there is time, with a life application. Jesus most often began with a life problem and then taught information.

People are most highly motivated to learn when the information will help them solve a problem or shed light on a puzzling situation. Research in human development supports the idea that people develop most rapidly when they struggle with significant problems.[9] God uses the problems and trials of life as a stimulus for spiritual growth (James 1:2-4). Tension arises when our lives get out of step with the standards of God's Word. Often the middle rail of our lives is out of alignment with the top rail of God's standards. When this happens, problems result. It makes sense for small-group methods to begin with the problems of life as a stimulus for serious Bible study.

Methods that begin with life tie together the two bottom rails. The learner is stimulated to *focus* on his or her personal life and is encouraged to interact with others in the group facing similar situations. This first step motivates the group to wrestle with the content of Scripture.

## Study the Bible

The Good News of the Bible takes on powerful significance when it is contrasted with the "bad news" of our lives.

God has given an authoritative Map that will help pilgrims get out of swamps of despondency, climb hills of discouragement, avoid dungeons of doubt, and delight in the beauty of Immanuel's Land. This Book even gives exciting glimpses of the City—the final destination. What a Book! Pilgrims may begin their small groups by sharing personal encouragements or painful situations, but they must study the Map in order to make sense of past experiences and to gain insights for the road ahead.

Pilgrims don't make up their own maps; they use the official Map of the King. So it is important for pilgrims to study carefully what the Map actually says and what it meant to the person who authored it. Pilgrims who use discovery Bible study methods don't make up their own meaning; they discover the objective truth that comes from God. Wise pilgrims don't study God's Word because they want to feel good. They study because they are searching for truth and ways to apply the truth. They know that merely sharing what the Map means to them may lead to misinterpretation and danger ahead. Wise pilgrims are serious students of the Word of God. Group methods must take time to *observe* what the Bible is actually saying—the big ideas of each verse, paragraph, chapter, or book. They also ask what the passage meant to the author and the original people who heard the message. This is *interpretation.*

But Bible study has a purpose beyond mere knowledge. Too often small groups begin and end without helping people understand the *personal implications* of the study. The method must not isolate the top rail from the two bottom rails. Neither is it enough to tie together only the top and the bottom rails. Some methods foster group involvement in understanding the content of Scripture (the bottom and top rails) but don't encourage people to struggle with implications for their personal lives (the middle rail).

**Apply the Truth**

Most maps become outdated and contain errors. But the Map God has given is never out of date and has no mistakes. The truth of God's Map is not measured by how many pilgrims find the right road or by how many get lost. Pilgrims don't create truth; they discover it. But knowing the truth of God's Word is not enough. Knowing the Word is a *means* for knowing and loving God. Group methods must help us not only to discover truth, but to put it into practice—this is application.

Knowing and believing the truth does not automatically result in correct application. Even the demons believe the truth, but they don't put it into action (James 2:14-26). Each group member must ask, "What difference should the Bible make in my life?" "What should I do about what I have learned in this passage?" Bible knowledge is wasted unless it is put into practice.

The correct application of the Bible will do two things: it will change the heart and change behavior. Changed behavior will grow naturally out of a Christlike character. Putting the Bible into action in our lives is not shallow behaviorism nor a legalistic obedience to rules. Jesus teaches that obedient behavior must come from the heart.[10] The pilgrim journey is both internal and external—the development of the heart and of obedient behavior. Good group methods will encourage Bible application to develop inner character and to change outward behavior.

This third step can take place at any time. Don't wait until the end of the session to struggle with Bible application. As soon as a Bible truth is understood it is appropriate to ask, "What would I be like if I really believed this?" "What would happen Monday morning if I put this principle into practice?" "What does this mean for my involvement in other people's lives?"

Through an understanding of the nature of persons we know that people are created in the image of God with great worth and potential to know and love him. We also know that people are fallen and disobedient, unable to apply the truth in their own power. The Spirit within us helps us to obey the Bible. Group members need to take time to pray for each other as they apply God's truth to their lives. Application is not just a small group educational technique. Application of Bible truth is a supernatural process. And we have supernatural resources. Group methods need to provide opportunity for people to avail themselves of the power of the Spirit.

We've looked at the purpose, nature, aims, and methods of healthy groups. In the rest of this book, we'll look at the practical implications of these foundations.

## Questions for Reflection

1. Think again about a small group you are involved in. What methods are used in your group? Do they change often? If so, is there a purpose for the change other than change itself?

2. Do the methods in your group's practice contribute to application of Bible truth? Give examples of ways that Bible truth has brought about changed living in yourself or others.

3. What ideas can you suggest for beginning your group Bible study with life needs? For applying Scripture to life?

4. As you observe various small groups, reflect on the way life and truth are tied together. Use your observations to strengthen your own group's practice of truth.

## Notes

1. The "rail fence model" was first developed by Ted Ward and Sam Rowen as a curriculum model for theological education by extension.
2. Galatians 6:17.

3. Romans 8:9.

4. 1 Corinthians 12:7.

5. John 3:1-21.

6. John 4:1-26.

7. Luke 10:25-37.

8. A good example of this method is when Jesus told his disciples to watch out for the yeast of the Pharisees in Mark 8:14-21.

9. In Chapter 3, "The Nature of Pilgrims," we discussed "disequilibration," a term that describes struggle with significant problems. Disequilibration is a foundational concept of Piaget's theory of cognitive development. See Barry J. Wadsworth, *Piaget's Theory of Cognitive Development* (New York: David McKay Co., 1971).

10. Mark 7:1-23 and also Isaiah 29:13.

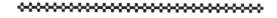

## *Why Small Groups Are Important to Me*

When I think of small groups, my mind takes me back to my college years—me and four of my buddies sitting on the floor of our dorm room talking about girls, God's will, the future, and the Bible. Although we weren't sophisticated, we were sincere. That relaxed approach has stayed with me ever since. The small group has given me a method of discovering God's wisdom from his Word within the context of a caring group.

Through various ministries, the method has stuck. As a youth pastor I gathered around me a group of teens who committed themselves to get together weekly for Bible study and prayer. My primary strategy as a college resident hall director was to provide opportunities for all my students to be involved in a small accountability group each week. In other contexts as a pastor, I have invited unchurched teens and adults into my home for Bible study and found them surprisingly open to God's Word.

In my present ministry as a college professor, I require all of my students who are entering Christian ministry to be involved in a class that includes participation in a weekly accountability group.

On a personal level, my wife and I have received great encouragement from a couples' sharing and prayer group that meets in our home.

Small group experiences focused on God's Word are essential to my personal growth and ministry. They keep me honest and intimate in my walk with God.

Gary Newton, Indiana

# 6

# Pilgrim Leaders

*How they enjoy the deference paid them on the streets,*
*and to be called "Rabbi" and "Master"!*
*Don't ever let anyone call you that.*
*For only God is your Rabbi*
*and all of you are on the same level, as brothers.*
MATTHEW 23:7-8, The Living Bible

WHY IS THE PILGRIMAGE SO DIFFICULT? UNCERTAINTIES, TEMPTA-tions, and hardships crowd the pathway and many pilgrims are waylaid by the Swamp of Despond, Doubting Castle, or the Hill of Difficulty. Why doesn't God provide pilgrims with the kind of leadership that assures an easy road?

God doesn't intend for pilgrims to march in lock-step, single-file formation with control-oriented leadership to make sure they don't get out of line. Yet many pilgrims seem to prefer the kind of leader who will tell them exactly what to do so they will never make a wrong turn, never be tempted to doubt, and never be forced into a battle with Satan. And some leaders would like to be benevolent dictators who take full responsibility for their pilgrims. But good leadership, while providing valuable help to pilgrims, is not dic- tatorial and cannot promise an easy road.

Competing theories of leadership range between the extremes of anarchy and totalitarianism. The controversy, to some extent, influences leadership in small groups. Some small group leaders assume that people need aggressive and creative leadership to set goals and provide inspiration. Others feel that the most effective leader acts as a catalyst or consultant to the group.[1] The tension can provoke heated arguments for Bible study groups.

On the one hand, a group member may say, "We have gifted people in our small group, but our leader structures every minute. We are so highly organized that there is no time to bring up the problems I'm facing in my life. Our leader doesn't think we know anything. There's a lot we could learn from each other if we had a chance to participate."

But a member from another group complains, "We'll never have a stimulating small group until we can get some dynamic leadership. Our leader is a real 'wimp.' He asks lots of questions about the Bible, but he never tells us any answers. When we face personal problems, he only asks us what *we* think. He never teaches or gives advice."

### Tensions in Leadership

*Leadership style* is one area of tension. Should the leader be authoritarian, telling the group what to do and who should do it? Or should the leader encourage a laissez-faire style, essentially allowing the group to function without a leader?

Some authoritarian leaders cite Scripture verses that describe the leader as a shepherd. Shepherds, they say, must take charge. They must plan, lead, organize, and control the sheep who really don't know where they are going. Laissez-faire leaders quote Scripture about servant leadership. Servants, they say, aren't supposed to tell people what to do; they merely do what others want them to do.

Some pastors won't allow small groups to meet in homes unless an approved leader is in charge of the group. Other groups continue for years without any designated leaders.

Some small group Bible studies have strict policy regarding lesson-preparation time, rules for participation, and prescribed goals for how much Scripture they will cover each week. This kind of group needs an authoritarian leadership style. Other groups decide their agenda each week, depending on the needs of the group. These groups do well with a laissez-faire kind of leader. Which leadership style is best?

Another area of friction concerns *leadership function*. What is the job of the leader? Is it to accomplish a task, or is it to build relationships within the group?

Task-oriented leaders understand their function as getting people to work toward a goal. The primary concerns of the task leader are management, delegation, and efficient use of time. Goals are measurable and predetermined.

Relationship-oriented leaders do not see the group as a task force, but as people with personal needs. The role of the relational leader is to mediate conflict within the group and to be an encourager. Accomplishing predetermined, measurable goals is considered an inappropriate role for relationship-oriented leaders.

Another area of disagreement has to do with *group focus*. Should the group encourage the freedom of the individual or the well-being of the group? Should individuals submit their personal rights for the good of the group? Or should the group serve the individual? Strong individualists will not work well in a small group, and when the leader or the group itself becomes a dictator, the individual will suffer. Groups that allow freedom of the individual do not function well with authoritarian leadership. But groups that hold individuals accountable to the group require more authoritarian leadership.

## Typical Solutions

A common solution to leadership tensions is to give people choices, providing opportunities for both task and relational groups. Highly goal-oriented people might join a task group such as the church finance committee. Such people generally prefer leaders who will get them through the agenda as efficiently as possible. "Relational" types might seek out serendipitous groups with leaders who provide for unexpected, unstructured interactions.

Another solution is to try to balance and blend the leadership extremes. Churches try not to be too authoritarian or too laissez-faire. They try to incorporate some relationship-building activities in task-oriented committee meetings. They suggest tasks for groups with a relationship-building focus. They seek to hold the individual accountable without being too overbearing.

But giving people choices and blending leadership functions avoids the question of which is best. Should we provide different leadership styles for people with different personality types, or should we seek a leadership style that is best for all people? Is the inclination toward a highly authoritarian or highly laissez-faire leadership style merely a personal preference, or is it a sign of sickness?

Good leadership can make a major contribution to the healthy development of pilgrims, and bad leadership can do tremendous harm. Leadership style cannot be based merely on the preference of the leader or the follower. Some people prefer unhealthy leadership styles.

Authoritarian leadership does little to strengthen pilgrims because they develop an unhealthy dependency on the leader and become weak. But laissez-faire leaders don't provide the help needed to meet the very real dangers of the journey. Allowing pilgrims to choose between authoritarian or laissez-faire leadership styles is no solution—both are dangerous.

Authoritarian leadership is usually task-oriented and concerned with controlling members of the group. The authoritarian leader can be kindly and paternalistic, but is often motivated by distrust and a desire for power. An authoritarian pastor may see himself as the monarch of the church, the father of "one big happy family."

He may attempt to control and manipulate the associate pastor and the youth director through fear. Church staff members are assumed to be lazy unless they are tightly controlled, and the laity is assumed to be headed toward heresy without the authority of the leader.

People often prefer authoritarian leadership because it frees them from taking responsibility for their decisions and from thinking for themselves. Because of the unhealthy tendency for many people to want to be dominated, small groups organized with a hierarchical chain-of-command may grow rapidly. But people in the group will become dependent on the leader and will not develop their full potential socially or spiritually. Eventually, tight control will lead to hostility. Authoritarian groups either stifle growth or incite rebellion. Authoritarian leaders trust themselves too much and trust others too little. They tend to disregard the fact that they are fallen sinners and that the people they work with are created in the image of God.

Laissez-faire leaders, on the other hand, have the opposite problem. They trust themselves too little and trust others too much. They tend to ignore the fact that they too are created in the image of God and that the people they serve are fallen. Their focus is on the freedom of individuals and relationship-building, but they fail to give direction and help. People whom God has gifted with abilities in leadership and teaching should use their gifts to strengthen others.

Laissez-faire leaders probably do less immediate harm than authoritarian leaders, but they do damage by not taking initiative to help hurting and lost pilgrims. Servant leaders must serve people, but they are ultimately responsible to God, and not to the group. People need servants who can give encouragement and wise advice from Scripture, even when they don't know they need such servants.

Pluralism is in vogue. Laissez-faire leaders may assume that truth is found inside each person and may be different for each one.

Thus they feel that the best leadership is the kind that gives freedom to the individual. The best leader, they say, is the one who gets out of the way and allows inner truth to grow in people. In these circles, it is not popular to believe in absolute truth. So while authoritarian leaders assume that they have a full understanding of all truth, laissez-faire leaders believe there is no objective truth.

Neither authoritarian leadership nor laissez-faire leadership is the answer to pilgrims' needs. A different model is needed.

## All Christians Are Leaders

All Christians are called to take initiative in helping others. All Christians are given spiritual gifts that are useful for building up others. When a person is responsible for influencing another person, that person is a leader. Therefore in an important sense, all Christians are called to be leaders. And all leaders are very much aware of the fact that they, too, are pilgrims.

How can all pilgrims be leaders? Isn't it dangerous to have so many chiefs? This sounds too radical. Romans 12:8 seems to suggest that only certain people have the gift of leadership. Those who have the gift of leadership are told to govern diligently. While some Christians are given special gifts in management and administration, the Bible also teaches that all Christians have responsibilities in serving, encouraging, contributing to the needs of others, and showing mercy. A person cannot say, "I have no responsibility for showing mercy because it isn't my gift." Some people may have extraordinary abilities in leadership and may be called to formal leadership tasks, but all Christians are encouraged to take the lead in using their gifts for the common good. Each person who influences another person is a leader, even if that person is not designated as the formal leader. Ephesians 4:7-13 teaches that *each* person has been given grace that is to be used to prepare God's people for works of service, to build up the body of Christ.

Designated leaders may have special organizational responsibilities, but often the most influential people in the group are not
the official leaders. God calls *all* his people to be a holy and royal
priesthood.[2] The priesthood of all believers means that every Christian has direct access to God and can minister to others. The Holy
Spirit is at work in the life of every Christian. If a person does not
have the Spirit of Christ, he does not belong to Christ (Rom. 8:9).
Christians don't have to go through "ordained" leadership in order
to approach God and serve others. Those who belong to the royal
priesthood are called to take initiative in using all their leadership
gifts to serve.

Experts who are highly trained in biblical languages, biblical
culture, and theology can provide valuable insights into the original meaning of Scripture. But every true Christian has the Spirit
of Christ living in him or her and can understand the basic meaning
of the Bible. Pilgrims do not need biblical experts to serve as
mediators because God can speak clearly to each believer through
his Word. The doctrine of the priesthood of all believers has astounding implications for pilgrim leaders.

Pilgrims most often travel in small groups, but they don't travel
like a herd of animals, blindly following a leader. Each pilgrim has
responsibilities to warn, encourage, and strengthen other pilgrims.
No pilgrim can be excused for wandering off the right path by
claiming, "The leader led me astray. It isn't my fault I got lost." Each
pilgrim is held accountable for his or her own actions. Pilgrims are
responsible to help each other, but pilgrims are ultimately not
accountable to other pilgrims or to pilgrim leaders. Each pilgrim is
accountable to God. While we must help each other and take
responsibility to influence through teaching, no pilgrim should be
controlled by another pilgrim. It is both sobering and exciting to
realize that all pilgrims are called to be leaders.

In small group Bible studies, there may be a designated leader
to facilitate discussion and to make sure the group begins and ends

on time. But no one in the group has the right simply to sit back and watch. Each member must be constantly on the alert for ways to be of help to others. Designated leaders of small groups must also see their task as allowing each person to be a leader.

If the leader is seen as the boss, it doesn't make sense to claim that all Christians are leaders. Only one person can be the boss. Chaos would result if everyone tried to boss everyone else around. But Christian leaders are not to be bosses. Jesus said, "You are not to be like that. Instead, the greatest among you should be like the youngest, and the one who rules like the one who serves" (Luke 22:26). Only as servant leaders can everyone be a leader.

**Leaders Do Not Control**

Pilgrims need to stick together. Traveling in groups is the way God intended pilgrims to overcome the Evil One and to evangelize those seeking the path. When people work together in groups, it is useful to designate certain people to be in charge of specific functions. Leaders with special gifts may be chosen to help the group through difficult times. A pilgrim leader who is an expert in Map-reading can help pilgrims who are confused about which path to take. Other pilgrim leaders who have had previous experiences with difficulties on the road can move to the front of the pilgrim band and lead the way. Effective pilgrim leaders lead through expertise in teaching and through modeling.

The Good Shepherd never drives his sheep with a whip. They willingly follow because he calls them by name and they know his voice. Jesus never forced people to follow him. Neither did he coerce them into the kingdom. Jesus led his followers through the authority of his teaching and through the example of his life.

Jesus called them together and said, "You know that the rulers of the Gentiles lord it over them, and their high officials exercise authority over them. Not so with you. Instead, whoever wants to become great among you must be your servant, and whoever wants to be first must be your slave—just as the Son of Man did not come to be served, but to serve, and to give his life as a ransom for many." Matthew 20:25-28

Neither the carrot stick of bribery nor the whip of force is appropriate for pilgrim leaders. The church in every culture is tempted to adopt unhealthy leadership styles. It is normal for leaders to want to exercise authority over others. Hundreds of examples can be given in North America, Africa, Europe, Asia, and South America of born-again Christian leaders who crave power over others. Local churches, denominations, and para-church organizations are too often characterized by leaders who fight for power. Many Christian leaders imitate *The Leadership Secrets of Attila the Hun*[3] rather than the teachings of Jesus. One chapter in that book is titled "The lust for leadership: You've got to want to be in charge." Jesus commanded that this not be so among Christians. A controlling leadership style in the church has done great harm to the kingdom. Nothing is clearer in Jesus' teaching than his repeated warning that leadership among his people is not to be modelled after the world's pattern. The lust to be in charge is from the Evil One. Authoritarian guru leaders in small group Bible studies can be very destructive. The pilgrim leader must be motivated by an overpowering love for the Lord and a strong desire to serve and to help pilgrims grow.

## Leading by Example

If leaders don't manage by controlling or exercising power over others, how can they lead? They cannot sit back, watching pilgrims wander through swamps. They must try to influence pilgrims.

It all goes back to the nature of persons. As we saw earlier, while people are created in the image of God with great potential, they are also fallen. Even Christian leaders have the tendency to be self-centered, power hungry, and oppressive. Many Christian books on leadership are based on pagan management theory with Bible verses tacked on.[4]

Today there is an urgent need for servant leaders, leaders who lead by example. Paul told Timothy and Titus that leaders must have a good reputation, be models of maturity in their homes, hold firmly to the trustworthy message, and be able to teach.[5] Yet most contemporary leaders are selected because they are well-educated, have charismatic personalities, and have a strong drive to accomplish tasks. While none of these characteristics are bad, neither are they necessary for leaders.

Jesus was a compelling leader because of his example. He taught the importance of prayer, not by demanding that his disciples pray for one hour every morning, but by praying regularly himself. He taught servant leadership, not by giving a lecture on the history and theology of servanthood, but by washing the feet of his disciples. Modeling is a powerful way to be an influential leader.

The home of the New Testament leader was to be a model of leadership. Elders were not told to lead workshops or write books on the ideal home. They were to *demonstrate* an ideal home. They weren't told to preach sermons on the importance of hospitality, but to be characterized as hospitable people.

## Leading by Teaching

Pilgrim leaders cannot be laissez-faire—they must try to influence others. Yet they cannot be dictators, forcing their influence on others.

One of the best ways to influence pilgrims without being dictatorial is to help them understand the content and the meaning of the Map. Leaders influence others by helping them know and apply God's truth. All New Testament leaders were to be characterized by an ability to teach (1 Tim. 3:2). Leaders were to hold firmly to the trustworthy message so they could encourage believers and refute error through teaching sound doctrine (Titus 1:9).

Leaders can't manipulate followers or coerce them into obedience; they must influence indirectly. Teachers do this as they challenge people to see their lives as measured by the Bible. Leaders can't force people to obey the Bible, but they are responsible for helping people to understand what it means to live in obedience to God's truth. Pilgrim leaders are guides and interpreters of the Map. They are never gurus, claiming themselves to be the source of truth.

## Leading through Vision

Leaders must have a sense of direction—a calling. Pilgrims need Spirit-gifted leaders who are non-coercive and non-manipulative. "If anyone sets his heart on being an overseer, he desires a noble task" (1 Tim. 3:1). Leaders know their Source and their Goal. They have a passionate sense of vision.

Too often, business-oriented management theory dominates Christian views of leadership. According to management theory, leaders need specific, measurable goals. "If we aim at nothing specific, we'll hit it every time." Or, "What gets measured gets done." But precise goals are alien for pilgrims who are facing unpredictable dangers on the road. There are too many precarious experiences along the path. Pilgrims must have a strong sense of direction and destination, but they are not specifically sure where the path will lead in the near future. Leaders who get bogged down with measurable, short-term objectives often miss unfolding opportunities that arise around them. By definition, measurable and predictable goals are not eternal! We are headed to a heavenly city. We are concerned with the inner character development of pilgrims. We are fighting for the souls of people. The most important things in life and in eternity are not measurable: "So we fix our eyes not on what is seen, but on what is unseen. For what is seen is temporary, but what is unseen is eternal" (2 Cor. 4:17).

Yet pilgrim leaders don't lack vision. Effective leaders must have an obsession for the glory of God and a passionate love for other people. They have a picture of how eternity can be different because of God's influence through them. They have a strategic vision for eternal goals and they know how to respond to the opportunities unfolding around them in light of that vision.[6] Christians may achieve excellence as managers and administrators and yet damage pilgrims. Good management can be a useful tool, but management should never be confused with leadership. Pilgrim leaders are people with a passionate love for God who use their spiritual gifts for developing other pilgrims.

Pilgrim leaders are also concerned to stir up a clearer sense of vision in other pilgrims. They study God's vision as explained in the Map of the Word. Their focus is not on short-term activity (such as "covering" a certain amount of material), but on the long-term development of people for the glory of God. Thus if a special need arises in a small group, they are free to shift the focus of that study in order to meet a need that may have eternal significance.

**The Task versus the Person**

The real task for pilgrim leaders is to love the Lord and love others. We usually think of tasks as projects or activities. A committee can be assigned the task of finding a new pastor or building a new church. A small group leader may visualize the task as attracting more people or covering a pre-set curriculum. The real task, however, is not carrying out activities but facilitating spiritual growth in people.

Authoritarian leaders may accomplish tasks by using people as means, or as cogs in a machine. This hinders the accomplishment of the real task—developing people. Laissez-faire leaders at the other extreme tend to be directionless, forgetting the needy world around them. God gave pilgrims a task to do—they are called to be the salt and light of the world and to make disciples in all nations.

We are faced with a dilemma. How can task-oriented leaders or people-oriented leaders accomplish anything of eternal significance? The dilemma can only be solved when we turn the problem around. We don't use people to accomplish tasks, nor do we focus exclusively on people, ignoring the task. We see the task as a means, not an end—a means for developing people. Leaders use important tasks as tools for developing pilgrims.

Effective leaders know that pilgrims are strengthened when they become involved in ministry. The task of evangelism and growth toward Christlikeness is both the means and the end of the pilgrimage. Yet pilgrim leaders are completely dependent on the grace of God to accomplish anything. Since the task is supernatural it can only be done through the supernatural power of the Lord working through us. Influential pilgrim leaders spend much time in prayer and in the study of the Word of God.

Pilgrim leaders are urgently needed in all levels of church life but especially in small groups.

**Questions for Reflection**
**1.** What kind of leadership styles have you observed in groups you have been a part of? How did these help or hinder the growth of group members?

**2.** What is your role in your small group? How does your role benefit the group?

**3.** Do you agree that all Christians are leaders? In what ways are you taking initiative to help others in your group?

**4.** Reflect on the implications that the doctrine of "the priesthood of all believers" might have for your group.

## Notes

**1.** A good discussion of the tension in leadership theory can be found in the article by Jack R. Gibb, "Dynamics of Educational Leadership" in William R. Lassey and Marshall Sashkin, *Leadership and Social Change,* third edition (San Diego: University Associates, 1983), pp. 188-202.

**2.** 1 Peter 2:5, 9; Exodus 19:6; Revelation 5:10.

**3.** Wess Roberts, *Leadership Secrets of Attila the Hun* (New York: Warner, 1987).

**4.** Even mature Christian leaders have remnants of their sinful nature and thus desire to exercise authority over others. Because leaders are corrupted by the Fall, power has the tendency to corrupt leaders even more.

**5.** 1 Timothy 3:1-10 and Titus 1:6-9.

**6.** The business world is seeing the need for strategic vision as illustrated in John Naisbitt's statement, "Strategic planning is worthless—unless there is first a strategic vision" in *Megatrends* (New York: Warner Books, 1982), p. 94. Too often businesses have had such precise objectives that they missed unpredicted unfolding opportunities around them. Christian books on leadership have been overly influenced by inadequate theories of management.

## *Why Small Groups Are Important to Me*

For me, living the Christian life without small groups would be like trying to breathe without lungs. Within the first ten days of my Christian journey, I was exposed to the great benefit of a face-to-face encounter with Christ, a significant circle of believers, and the text of the Scripture—all at once. I was a freshman at college and during the first week of school another student invited me to come to his room after supper. It was his custom, and that of his friends, to read the Bible together, commenting on how the text spoke to each person, and then praying. So my first exposure to small groups was on a daily basis. Perhaps that first encounter made a permanent life-changing imprint on my life, one from which I happily will never recover. Our first experiences in the new life, especially those in the first few weeks, are like a child's first experiences upon entering this world. A deep imprinting takes place. How fortunate I was to be imprinted with the need to ground the Christian message in a real fellowship that could hold me accountable.

Now, after thirty-four years of following Jesus, I look back with almost overwhelming gratitude to the rich treasures God has given me through the many small groups I have enjoyed. I think there has only been one year out of all those years that I, and now my wife, have been without the benefit of such a fellowship. Some of these groups have been with exclusively committed people. Other groups have been a mixture of believers and not-yet-Christians (by far the most exciting context). But for all the rich opportunities I have had to hear profound expositions of the Scripture, there remains in my mind no deeper encounter with the Word of God than that which I have experienced in a small group. There the Word takes flesh once again and Jesus becomes real.

Not that it is easy! I remember one night when a visitor told our group that they were completely insensitive to the fact that I was a hurting person. Even *I* did not know that. And it was through the group that I came to grips with my own need for healing. On another occasion, when we were celebrating the Lord's Supper, our relationships were so tangled and broken that one after another protested his or her inability to celebrate the Supper. So we gave ourselves a full week to mend our relationships and came together again with deep joy.

So I hope that in heaven there will be a place for a few of us to gather to enjoy a small group Bible study. Perhaps then we won't need a Bible studyguide!

R. Paul Stevens, Vancouver

# 7

# Benefits and Pitfalls

---

*Let him who cannot be alone beware of community.*
*Let him who is not in community beware of being alone.*
DIETRICH BONHOEFFER, Life Together

E ACH PILGRIM IS INDIVIDUALLY ACCOUNTABLE TO GOD AND needs time to cultivate this relationship, but pilgrims also need other pilgrims. We cannot be like Ignorance in *Pilgrim's Progress* who "preferred to walk alone." He missed out on the benefits of walking in the company of other pilgrims. That was his downfall, and so "it went ill with him at last."

When Hopeful was tempted to sleep on the Enchanted Ground, Christian rebuked him and reminded him of the dangers of that place. Hopeful accepted Christian's reprimand saying, "I admit my error. If I had been alone here, I would have slept and run the danger of death. Two are better than one; your company has been a mercy to me."[1]

John Wesley made small groups a cornerstone of his revival movement because he believed solitary religion "is a phrase no more consistent with the Gospel than holy adulterers. The Gospel of Christ knows of no such religion."[2]

Small groups extend unique benefits to pilgrims. But there are also pitfalls to avoid in small-group settings. Let's look first at the benefits small groups provide.

## Benefits

### Growth

Through small groups, pilgrims can be a means of grace—a mercy—to one another. God created us to thrive in community. Being in a small group of caring people opens up a whole new dimension of growing that can't take place individually or in large groups.

For the serious believer, being in a small group is hardly optional. No one in his right mind would attempt to climb Mount Kilimanjaro on his own, and no Christian in his right mind would attempt to walk the Christian journey alone. Members of small groups are like mountain climbers roped together for the ascent. Climbing in groups enables pilgrims to achieve new heights they would never see on their own.

Spiritual growth, like emotional and mental growth, doesn't take place in a vacuum: It is fostered and enhanced by interaction. God has given gifts to each of us that can contribute to the growth of others. But these gifts often lie dormant. In small groups, we can help each other "fan into flame" the gifts God has given. To do this, we need to know each other well and be committed to learning from each other.

### Belonging

All of us belong to small groups in the various stages of our lives—our families, scout troops, soccer teams, bowling leagues, PTA, book discussions, etc. We are born with a need for belonging and find ourselves drawn to groups where we can establish relationships and work on a common task. Considering all the groups people give attention to, it makes a lot of sense to make a commitment to a group whose goal is growing in Christ—the ultimate purpose of life. Each Christian needs to be surrounded by cheerleaders and challengers to accomplish this goal.

A small group is a place where you are missed if you don't come. It creates a setting where needs can be met on a personal, practical level. It's a place where we can "carry each other's burdens" in obedience to Scripture. Where, in the average church, do people have an opportunity to discuss their real concerns—job insecurities, ethical dilemmas, prodigal children? In large group settings, we don't even know one another's burdens, much less how to help carry them.

In the increasingly mobile, urban society we live in, settings where pilgrims can experience a sense of belonging are more important than ever. Families are fragmented and neighbors hardly know each other. Many jobs are dehumanizing, contributing further to a sense of alienation. Hours of television viewing reduce time spent in conversation and personal relationships. In our bankrupt society, healthy small groups can meet a growing hunger for belonging.

## Encouragement

The encouragement that people receive in the church is often similar to that of a store clerk who hands you a receipt and says, "Have a nice day." It's impersonal and perfunctory. Shaking hands with people in the church foyer is nice, but it doesn't begin to meet the core needs of the soul.

John Wesley described the importance of the small cell groups he organized in this way:

> Many now happily experienced that Christian fellowship which they had not so much as an idea before. They began to "bear one

another's burdens" and naturally to "care for each other." As they had daily a more intimate acquaintance with, so they had a more endeared affection for, each other.[3]

Being in a small group puts us in an environment where others can care for us deeply and where we can feel that care. It's like being a part of a caring, praying "family." This is important on every level—emotionally, physically, and spiritually.

Caring for *physical* needs may be the most obvious level of care—bringing in food when someone is sick, babysitting for a weary mother, or lending a hand to clean a flooded basement. This kind of caring may seem ordinary and mundane, but it's a powerful expression of love and often opens the way for ministering on other levels.

Rejoicing with those who rejoice and weeping with those who weep is the biblical way of caring on the *emotional* level. How can this happen unless pilgrims know each other's joys and sorrows? Sustained, consistent caring won't take place in large groups. It takes a small group where pilgrims can make progress reports (or admit to going backwards) and then receive the support of other group members to persevere in the journey.

Physical and emotional caring are crucial, but by themselves they are inadequate. *Spiritual* caring encourages pilgrims toward their ultimate purpose—glorifying God and becoming like Christ. John Wesley's groups asked the penetrating question, "How is your soul?" As group members look together at the standard of God's Word, they can encourage each other to take steps that will bring them closer to that standard. This is encouragement at the deepest level.

### Life Application

Small groups reduce the scale of the sanctuary to living room size. People come face to face instead of looking at the backs of heads lined up in rows. The focus becomes person-to-person in an atmosphere where interpersonal relationships can flourish. As trust develops, pilgrims acknowledge and share burdens. Together, they celebrate victories.

In a sermon, application of Scripture is necessarily "generic," but in a small group Bible study, Scripture can be applied specifically and individually. Feedback is immediate and appropriate to specific concerns. George Webber comments,

> People who have listened politely to sermons for years, when they gather together to listen to God's word from the Bible, are most likely to squirm in the face of honest confrontation, and only with difficulty can they brush aside the demands upon their lives.[4]

According to pollster George Barna, most Americans own a Bible, but few read it. "Until people see the Bible as a practical guidebook for their everyday existence, it will probably remain on the shelf."[5]

Small groups are an ideal place to help pilgrims take the Bible off the shelf and use it to find their bearings for whatever fork in the road they are facing. Others in the group may have come to that same fork previously. In the interactive, personal environment of the small group, they can recount their experience, showing how the Map and other pilgrims helped them along the way.

God delights to work through people. Fellow pilgrims are often the means by which God's grace reaches needy people. Richard Lovelace expresses it this way:

> *Among the most vital means of grace are other Christians.* Neither the Bible nor the sacraments will leave the shelf or the sanctuary to rescue a Christian who is too discouraged or backslidden to pray or worship. But a concerned brother or sister will do this again and again![6]

One way to mold a group into a true fellowship is to allow time for each member to share his or her personal history. This is a way to get to know group members so that prayer and encouragement can be more focused and specific. It's also a benefit to each group member to see God's faithfulness in individual lives and to learn from other pilgrims' experiences in the walk of faith.

## Pitfalls

While small groups provide enormous benefits for pilgrims on their journey, there are also potential small-group pitfalls to be avoided along the way.

### Doctrinal Heresy

Many pastors are genuinely concerned that groups without professional leadership will go astray. Certainly, there are examples of groups that have gone off the deep end and even become cultish. (But the same can be said for entire churches that have been led into heresy by an authoritarian pastor.)

Small groups that have a strong sense of their ultimate purpose and that plan their aims, activities, and methods accordingly will avoid heresy. The key is to let Scripture be the King—the authority and guide—of every group. And God has given the Holy Spirit to live in each group member as a teacher and guide. "I will ask the Father, and he will give you another Counselor to be with you forever—the Spirit of truth. . . . The Counselor . . . will teach you all things and will remind you of everything I have said to you" (John 14:16, 26).

Dr. John White recognizes the danger of groups going off on a tangent or even into doctrinal heresy, but he comments:

Anything that is good has its disadvantages and dangers, and unless we take risks we will never make progress. If ever there is to be something that the world will recognize as not *of* itself, it will be the phenomenon of Christians meeting to pray and to love one another in a practical way. It is not the big, well-dressed Sunday morning congregational service that attracts sinners but the warm fellowship of the house group.[7]

## Superficiality

Groups tend to stay on a safe level where members talk about sports, weather, studies, or jobs—carefully sidestepping matters of the heart. Even in Bible study, it's tempting to stay on an informational level, asking what the Bible says without asking, *so what?*

When no one rocks the boat with a challenge or no one admits to problems or pain, groups stay on a superficial level and eventually they dry up. The first step in the Alcoholics Anonymous program is the admission, "I am an alcoholic." In our small groups for pilgrims we need to say, "I am a sinner."

Critical reflection on Scripture and life is the remedy for superficiality. Contrasting the bad news of our lives with the good news of the Scriptures is the way to go deeper. Pilgrims make progress when they continually tie together Scripture and life.

## Personality Conflicts

When pilgrims travel together, they're bound to learn a lot about each other. But they won't always like what they learn! Some pilgrims are too talkative and domineering; others are too critical or dramatic; some lack commitment to the pilgrim group and are always late. Friction is inevitable.

Don't be afraid of problems between pilgrims! Crises are opportunities for growth. That's why you join a pilgrim group—to grow. It's true that small groups often bring out personality problems, but they also provide one of the best places for working those problems out. Problems are a normal part of growing together—

even a necessary part. Problems shouldn't be surprising since all of us who come together in groups are needy people. Use problems the way God intended—as a means toward growth.

There are many helpful resources for enhancing group dynamics.[8] But when you think about "how to handle problem people," remember that those very people can provide you with opportunities for significant growth.

In his book *Life Together*, Dietrich Bonhoeffer said,

> Every Christian community must realize that not only the weak need the strong, but also that the strong cannot exist without the weak. The elimination of the weak is the death of fellowship.[9]

## Varied Expectations

Group members come together with various ideas about what they expect from a small group. Some are ready for intense confrontation and accountability. Others want a measured pace with a lot of individual space. Some members are ready to make huge time and energy commitments. Others see the small group as one of many activities in their lives.

The important thing is to have an understanding together as you begin your group about what you expect and what you see as the group's purpose. Some groups find it helpful to draw up a formal covenant or contract.[10] Other groups simply talk together about what will work best for them and come to an understanding about the level of commitment expected.

One caution to keep in mind is that most groups aren't equipped to do therapy for serious problems. One person's problems shouldn't become the focus of the whole group. Someone with a serious problem can expect support from a group, but shouldn't depend on the group for therapy. Actual counseling should be done one-on-one or in specific group-therapy situations.

## Excessive Authority

Some people are wary of becoming part of a small group because they fear the kind of domination that can develop in such a setting. In the 1970s, many groups that ministered to the counterculture developed highly structured groups under strong, authoritarian leadership. They felt this was necessary because of the pagan background of the converts. The so-called "shepherding movement" of the 1970s and early 1980s is an example of this kind of authoritarian leadership. Individuals were told to "get under the authority" of mature Christians to whom they were expected to submit. These leaders expected to control even the most personal decisions of their followers. The movement resembled a religious Gestapo that investigated every detail of people's lives. Many members of these authoritarian groups were "burned" and continue to be afraid of small groups because of their experience.

Excessive authority is a pitfall that all pilgrims should watch for. Pilgrim leaders, as described in chapter 6, need to encourage diversity in groups, recognizing that each pilgrim is uniquely gifted. Pilgrim leaders must challenge sin but should allow room for disagreement over issues not clearly decided by Scripture. It's tragic when everyone in a group begins thinking, sounding, acting, and even looking alike. Diversity is the beauty of Christ's body expressed in groups.

## Inward Focus

Sometimes groups put so much energy into building a strong community that they become ingrown and selfish. Others see the group as an impenetrable clique.

The most obvious remedy for this pitfall is to deliberately develop outreach and service ministries. The Church of the Saviour in Washington D.C. forms each of its groups around a service task or mission. Groups meet weekly for Bible study, prayer, and personal sharing, but they also discuss mission strategies and support each other in reaching out. As members minister to others, they discover that they are even more united by this common goal.

The question of "open" versus "closed" groups is a difficult one. A group may be concerned about appearing selfish or cliquish if it limits its membership. On the other hand, when a group gets too large, the unique aspects of small group life are lost. Eight to twelve people is an optimal size. Beyond that number, it's difficult to involve and care for each person the way small groups are meant to do.

Some churches require all small groups to change membership each year. That avoids the problem of cliquishness, but it may introduce other problems. Some group members don't feel comfortable getting to know a new set of people each year. They have established a strong sense of community, and they resent being told that they have to split up. On the other hand, thinking a group must go on forever is unhealthy, too. Each group is unique, and no rules can apply to each situation. A group that is sensitive to the needs of its members and also reaches out in ministry to others will be healthy and receptive to God's guidance for continuity. When the time does seem right to disband, groups can plan regular reunions to maintain those relationships that have become so important.

Benefits and pitfalls—we've seen the advantages small groups provide and also the dangers to be avoided. Pilgrims will find invaluable support and encouragement in small group settings. Avoiding pitfalls along the way will make those small groups even more beneficial as pilgrims grow together toward Christlikeness.

### Questions for Reflection
**1.** Has there been a time in your life when you tried to go it alone without the help of other believers? Describe a time when the help of other Christians has been a means of grace to you.

**2.** Identify some of the markers in your life when you have experienced significant spiritual growth. Did other believers have a part in that growth?

**3.** Does your small group provide the benefits described in this chapter? If not, what can you do to strengthen it?

**4.** What pitfalls have you experienced in small groups? What safeguards can help you to avoid these in the future?

### Notes

1. John Bunyan, *The Pilgrim's Progress*, as retold by Gladys N. Larson (Chicago: Covenant Press, 1978), p. 67.

2. Quoted in James A. Davies, "Small Groups: Are They Really So New?" *Christian Education Journal*, Volume V, Number 2, p. 44.

3. John Wesley, "A Plain Account of the People Called Methodists" in *Works*, VIII, 254.

4. George W. Webber, *The Congregation in Mission* (New York: Abingdon Press, 1964), p. 82.

5. Reported in Bob Chuvala, "Christian Update" in *Christian Herald*, July/August 1989, p. 6.

6. Richard F. Lovelace, *Renewal as a Way of Life* (Downers Grove, Ill.: InterVarsity, 1985), p. 178.

7. John White, *Flirting with the World* (Wheaton, Ill.: Harold Shaw Publishers, 1982), p. 141.

8. See Em Griffin's *Getting Together* (InterVarsity) and *Group Talk!* by Ed Stewart and Nina Fishwick (Regal Books).

9. Dietrich Bonhoeffer, *Life Together* (New York: Harper and Row, 1969).

10. For help in formulating a group covenant, see Roberta Hestenes, *Using the Bible in Groups* (Westminster Press), chapter 2, or Lyman Coleman, *Training Manual for Small Group Leaders*, (Serendipity House), p. 49.

## *He Had No Small Group*

Every few months his wife would suggest that they join a couples' Bible study. And every time he had a good reason not to: he had too many sales appointments in the evening; he didn't know who the others in the group would be; he was afraid the leader would put him on the spot and he'd be embarrassed. And so he had no small group.

Then the storm struck. Devastating in its fury, it was perhaps not so different from the storms that often strike families with teenaged children. But to him it felt like the very end of life itself. The anguish was unrelenting, and his aloneness was profound. His wife, who might have provided some measure of comfort and courage, became in his mind the person to blame for the disaster. A Christian for many years, he could have prayed. But he was hurting so terribly that he couldn't. He feared for his sanity and for his survival. His days were agonizing, and his nights were filled with terror, month after month after month.

The storm is over now, and in the kindness of God the wreckage has been rebuilt. There may be other storms ahead; life's like that. But now he's in a small group. It will probably make a difference.

Anonymous

# 8

# Discovering
# the Map

*The Bible was never intended to be a book
for scholars and specialists only. From the very beginning
it was intended to be everybody's book,
and that is what it continues to be.*

F.F. BRUCE

PILGRIMS AREN'T WANDERING NOMADS. THEY HAVE A DESTINATION and a purpose. How do they know the way to reach their goal? God has given an authoritative Map for the journey. Pilgrims can help each other to understand and interpret that Map.

Small groups provide an ideal setting for discussion focused on the Bible. But what's so great about discussion? Isn't there a place for a good lecture? Yes! We need effective Bible expositors who can clearly proclaim the Word of God. But to complement this kind of teaching (and to reach lost pilgrims where they are) we need interactive learning that takes place in small groups.

Something happens in small group Bible study that doesn't happen individually or in large congregations. Bible study comes alive when believers look together at a passage and struggle to discover its implications for life. Together, they uncover truths that no commentary or pastor could ever teach them. William Barclay says,

It is only when truth is discovered that it is appropriated. When a man is simply told the truth, it remains external to him and he can quite easily forget it. When he is led to discover the truth himself it becomes an integral part of him and he never forgets.[1]

It is not enough for the leader of a group to be the discoverer who then shares his or her insights with the group. Each participant needs to experience the joy and benefits of personal discovery.

Often, the very people who most need to study the Bible are not in churches. They need to be reached in the workplace, in dorm rooms, and in homes. And what about the pewsitters who take in sermons week after week? They too need an opportunity to participate actively in discovering the Word of God for themselves. The difference between listening to a sermon and discovering Bible truth for yourself is like the difference between watching a skiing event on television and actually skiing the exhilarating slopes of a mountain. Bible study isn't meant to be a spectator sport.

## Discovery Bible Study

What makes for an effective Bible study? There are many approaches, but one of the most effective for group settings is *discovery* Bible study (or inductive Bible study). The goal of discovery study is to take the Bible text seriously and discover its implications for our lives.

A group can do this by encouraging each member to ask:
1. What is my life situation? *(focus)*
2. What does the text say? *(observation)*
3. What does it mean? *(interpretation)*
4. What does it mean to me? *(application)*
5. What am I going to do about it? *(action)*

The first kind of question helps group members to *focus* on the theme of the passage as it relates to their present lives. It also helps a group to begin talking and feeling comfortable together before

getting into the actual passage. As people reflect on their frustra-
tions, successes, satisfactions, or failures, they are more motivated
to dig into Scripture. In a study of Psalm 23, this approach question
might be, "What situations in your life this week have made you
aware of your need for God's care?"

Some groups are tempted to skip *observation* questions, going
right into interpretation and application. But that can lead to some
strange interpretations! Ronald Leigh cautions,

> Many times a person has a lot of trouble figuring out what a
> Bible passage means because he has not first done the work of
> carefully and objectively observing exactly what the passage
> says.[2]

Observe the "who, what, where, and when" of the passage first;
then you can interpret and apply it. It is possible, though, to overdo
this kind of question by asking it too often or asking questions that
are too obvious. Strong observation questions should help you to
look at the entire passage to find things like comparisons, contrasts,
and repetitions. For instance, an observation question for Psalm 23
might say, "Find all the terms that emphasize the pastoral setting
of the psalm." Or, "Find all the verbs in the psalm that describe
God's action as a good shepherd."

*Interpretation* questions ask for careful thinking about the implications of a passage. These include questions like, "What do you
think the psalmist meant by . . ." or "What does this tell us about
God's nature?" Lively interpretation questions can help you dig
out the meaning of the passage and the principles that emerge from
it. Interpretation questions are more open-ended than observation
questions and often have more than one good answer. During the
course of an actual Bible study, observation and interpretation
questions will often be mingled together.

*Application* questions ask, "What does this mean for me? How
should my life be changed because of what I understand from this

passage?" The question might be, "In what ways do you need God's shepherding care today?" You begin to think about how the passage could relate to your specific needs. Application questions don't always need to come at the end of a study. Whenever truth confronts life, it's appropriate to tie the two together with an application question.

*Action* questions ask, "So what? What are you going to do about it?" The point of studying and understanding Scripture is to be changed by it. We should feel a strong tension between the standard of Scripture and the actuality of our lives. Action questions need to pull these two realities together in a way that will motivate us to change the way we live. For example, "What area of your life will be different this week because of your trust in God's shepherding care?" If a verbal response is uncomfortable at this point, suggest that each person write down a response, or at least reflect quietly about it for a moment.

## Studyguides to the Rescue

Perhaps you're wondering, "How can I make all of that happen in my Bible study group?" It's true that asking good questions takes skill and hard work. You can learn to do it, but it will take a great deal of practice. There are a number of books to help you in that process.[3]

Another option that works well for many groups is the use of a Bible studyguide with questions designed to help you interact with the Bible in the discovery approach described above. Many excellent guides are available and you can adapt them to fit your group's needs.[4] These guides fall under three general categories: Bible book studies, topical studies, and character studies. Balance and variety are important for your group. After you've gone through a couple New Testament books, you may want to get into an Old Testament book like Genesis, Psalms, or Amos. Or, you may want to try a topical guide on prayer, relationships, or discipleship. Character

studies from both the Old and New Testaments will provide interesting examples for your group to learn from. Periodically, your
group may want to go back to a basic, introductory study for the
benefit of newcomers in the group.

A word of caution, though . . . Make sure the studyguide you
choose leads your group into interaction with the Bible. The term
"studyguide" can apply to a number of products that don't do that.
Some products are guides to an author's book rather than guides
to the Bible. This is fine if you want to study that book. But if it's
Bible study you're after, select carefully. Other so-called guides
function more like commentaries about Scripture, but they don't
provide much opportunity for you to discover Bible truths for
yourself. They are really sermons, with a few questions tacked on
at the end. These products do not encourage group discussion or
discovery Bible study.

Be aware, too, of the difference between deductive and inductive
Bible study. Deductive study begins with a premise (such as "God
is holy") and seeks to prove it from various parts of Scripture.
Inductive study (or discovery study) looks at a whole passage,
from beginning to end. The goal is to discover what the Scripture
says for itself and then to draw principles that emerge from the
facts of the text. A quick look at the number of references in each
study will often give a clue about the kind of study it is. A deductive
study will cite numerous Scriptures, treating each one briefly. Most
inductive studies stay in one passage and examine it in depth.

For beginning groups, the inductive method provides some
safeguards. For one thing, group members will not be asked to hop
around Scripture, which can be extremely confusing and embarrassing to novices. Most important, inductive study encourages
interpretation of a text within its context, protecting against the
heresies that can result from "proof-texting." It also provides a
Bible study pattern that anyone can easily adopt for personal study.

Some groups, though, may want the integrative approach that
deductive Bible study provides. Mature groups can use this ap-

proach but should be aware of the problems that can emerge from proof-texting.

## Guidelines for Leaders

A discovery Bible study group is not a "class" but a team of researchers studying a passage together. A study that is leader-centered tends to make the leader rather than the Scripture the authority for the group. One way to avoid this is to rotate leadership, keeping in mind that the leader is not the teacher, but the question-asker. The leader for the day is not the lecturer and does not need to be an expert on the passage. His or her role is to guide the group's discussion. The person who leads the study usually receives the greatest benefit, so that is all the more reason to encourage each member to have this opportunity. Good study-guides are the key to rotating leadership because they provide questions that lead the group into the Bible for answers.

Whether you rotate leadership or have one single leader, some general guidelines will help you to keep your group on track. Remember, though, that each group is unique, so be flexible and adapt these guidelines to fit your group.

• Relax! Take seriously the responsibility of leading your group, but don't take yourself too seriously. Pray, committing your group members and your study to the Lord.

• Prepare thoroughly so that you will be able to pace the study and keep it on target. Read the passage through a number of times so you are thoroughly familiar with it. Go through each question carefully, rewording and adapting as necessary.

• Create a comfortable atmosphere for your group. Make sure chairs are arranged so that everyone in the group can see each other. Pay attention to details like temperature, lighting, and eliminating distractions. This may mean leaving the telephone off the hook.

- Begin and end on time.
- Start the study with a brief prayer, asking for God's guidance. If you ask another group member to pray, be sure to get his or her permission beforehand. The same is true for asking others to read the Bible out loud. Ask for volunteers rather than reading around the circle.
- Encourage each person to participate, but don't put anyone on the spot. Almost every group has people who are predominantly talkers and others who are more comfortable as listeners. The challenge is to get the talkers listening and the listeners talking! Show appreciation for what each one says. Wait expectantly for quiet ones to speak. Occasionally you might say, "John, you have some good ideas on this subject. What do you think?"
- Avoid clichés and resist the temptation to overspiritualize or overapply. Don't say more than the Bible says!
- Ask! Don't tell. If someone asks you a question, expecting you to be the "answer-person," turn it into a question for the group, or point to the text. If it's a question you or someone else can't answer, don't be afraid to say, "I don't know. Let's study that this week and talk about it next time we meet."
- If someone comes up with a heretical idea, don't panic and don't feel responsible to correct it instantly. It will probably die a natural death without your help. You can gently ask, "Where do you find that in the passage?" Remember, the text is the authority and the Holy Spirit is your teacher. The goal of your study is to help each person discover the truth of Scripture personally.
- To avoid lengthy tangents, learn to say, "Well, back to the text . . ." or "The next question asks . . ." Of course sometimes there will be crucial needs that should be addressed immediately. And sometimes a group's most treasured moments grow out of a so-called tangent. So be sensitive to people's needs and the Holy Spirit's prompting in deciding whether to move on or to respond to a current need.

## Guidelines for Group Members

A few guidelines that all group members understand and agree to will help your group function smoothly. You will want to review these guidelines each time your group begins a new study.

• Stick to the passage under discussion. There is usually more than enough to glean from the passage at hand, and skipping around can be confusing.

• Don't talk too much or too little. The goal is one hundred percent participation. If you tend to dominate discussion, make a special effort to hold back and encourage others to participate. If you are naturally quiet, realize that you have unique perspectives to add to the study. You and the other group members will profit by hearing these ideas verbalized.

• Avoid tangents. Save interesting side-issues and talk about them over coffee after the study. Of course there are always some crucial exceptions but generally stick to the text.

• Don't criticize other churches or denominations. Keep the goal of the study group in mind, and don't detract from it.

## The Most Important Ingredient

There really isn't any "recipe" for an effective Bible study. Adapt, expand, and be flexible. The most important ingredient is personal discovery.

Bible study is not just for experts. In fact, "ordinary" group members often minister better to each other than does an expert. As C.S. Lewis explained,

> The expert sees the whole subject, by now, in such a different light that he cannot conceive what is really troubling the pupil; he sees a dozen other difficulties which ought to be troubling him but aren't ... The fellow pupil can help more than the master because he knows less."[5]

Studies led by scholars with degrees in Hebrew or Greek are not necessarily good discussions. Such experts usually feel compelled to teach the group rather than letting individuals discover for themselves what the Bible says. Of course there is a place for sermons and for teaching, but the unique benefit of small group Bible study is personal discovery.

Educator Thomas Groome suggests, "Don't tell very much at all. Ask great questions."[6] That's what discovery Bible study is all about.

You can facilitate growth-producing personal discovery in your group. And you can trust the Holy Spirit to teach and convict as you follow the Map together.

### Questions for Reflection

**1.** Describe a time when you discovered a truth for yourself rather than being told it. How did it happen? What was the effect of it in your life?

**2.** Does your Bible study include all the elements of discovery study (focus, observation, interpretation, application, and action)? If not, what steps can you take to include these elements?

**3.** What material does your small group use? If you use a study-guide, does it help the group to interact actively with Scripture?

**4.** How would you describe your study group—as a class or as a team of researchers? What's the difference?

### Notes

1. William Barclay, quoted in Oletta Wald, *The Joy of Discovery in Bible Study* (Minneapolis: Augsburg, 1975), p. 8.
2. Ronald W. Leigh, *Direct Bible Discovery* (Nashville: Broadman, 1982), p. 59.

**3.** If you are interested in writing your own questions, see *How to Lead Small Group Bible Studies* (NavPress, 1987). Another book to help you learn and understand the inductive Bible study method is Carolyn Nystrom's *Lord, I Want to Have a Quiet Time* (Shaw Publishers, 1984). Also see *Group Talk* by Ed Stewart and Nina Fishwick (Regal Books, 1987) and *Leading Bible Discussions* by James Nyquist and Jack Kuhatschek (InterVarsity, 1985).

**4.** Among the many excellent guides are: *Fisherman* and *Network Bible Studies* by Harold Shaw Publishers, *Lifeguide Bible Studies* by InterVarsity Press, *Neighborhood Bible Studies* by Tyndale House, *Mastering the Basics* by Serendipity, and *Workshop Bible Studies* by Zondervan. See appendix of this book for a sample discovery Bible study.

**5.** C.S. Lewis, *Reflections on the Psalms* (New York: Harcourt, Brace, & World, Inc., 1958), pp. 1-2.

**6.** Thomas Groome, lecture given at Wheaton Graduate School, "Educating for a Lived Faith," November, 1984. See appendix listing of his book, *Christian Religious Education.*

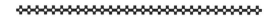

## *Why Small Groups Are Important to Me*

My own walk with God was launched by two small InterVarsity groups on my campus, one that met every day to pray and one that met weekly for Bible study. These groups were Christianity in front-line action. We prayed for ourselves, our growth, and our witness. On our campus, prayer was the lifeline to survival. In Bible study discussions, I first gained the thrill of discovering God's truth for myself. Over forty years since then, I have tried to maintain my spiritual vitality and walk with Christ by participating in community and church small groups.

Jim Reapsome, Illinois

# 9

# Pointing Pilgrims
# to the Path

*Suppose a number of persons were to take it
into their heads that they had to defend a lion.
There he is in the cage, and here come
all the soldiers of the army to fight for him.
Well, I should suggest to them that they should kindly
stand back, open the door, and let the lion out.
I believe that would be the best way of defending him.
And the best "apology" for the gospel is to let the gospel out.*
CHARLES SPURGEON

O UR INTEREST IN SMALL GROUP MINISTRIES BEGAN WHEN WE
were living on the campus of Michigan State University. We had
completed a rewarding term of missionary service in Nigeria and
now found ourselves with a year of furlough and new challenges.
As we looked around, our new setting seemed more "pagan" than
anything we had encountered in Nigeria. How could we reach out
to this needy place?

We heard about a "Neighborhood Bible Study Seminar" being
offered in a local church and decided to attend.[1] That was the
beginning of an on-going commitment to outreach evangelism
through small groups.

## Why Small Groups for Evangelism?

What is it about small groups that make them such appropriate settings for outreach and evangelism?

• Groups provide settings where sustained, personal interaction can take place. This is not a "hit and run" approach! Continuing exposure to Christianity is important for people who are deciding whether or not to make a commitment to Jesus Christ. Small group outreach is *responsible evangelism*.

• Through small group interaction, we can take seriously the *unique needs of individuals*. As discussion takes place, those needs become apparent and can be addressed. This can't happen in large group settings, and the result is that we often give answers to unasked questions. Small groups help us "scratch where it itches."

• Groups are a *natural way* to introduce people to Christianity. Most of us belong to groups of some kind—parenting groups, book discussion groups, financial investment groups, computer-users' groups, etc. It makes sense to form a group for studying the Bible together, too.

• Small groups can meet in *familiar, non-threatening places*—a dorm room, a favorite restaurant, a living room, or an office lounge. People who would never go with you to a church building might be happy to accept an invitation to your home.

• A small group provides a *more comfortable setting* for talking about Christ. This is the understood agenda, and the group will expect to discuss it. Others in the group will contribute to the discussion, too, so you don't have to be the expert or the answer-person. Christians will sharpen their abilities to witness and non-Christians can bring into focus the issues at stake.

• Through group study, members will *learn a pattern* for individual study. They will soon realize that there is much more to learn, and the group study will guide their personal search for truth.

• Small groups provide a welcoming environment where people can *feel they belong.* Fellowship is a fundamental need within each of us—just as important as food and drink. A group that finds ways to meet this need will be almost irresistible.

• Small groups have a powerful *effect on relationships,* too. Fragmented neighborhoods come together, office workers learn to care about each other, and students on a campus form a new bond.

## How Does It Work?

Suppose you want to reach out to friends and acquaintances around you—how do you go about it? One way is to host a coffee or some other social event where you invite friends to come and hear about the possibility of being in a small group Bible study.

Who do you invite? Resist the temptation to search out all the Christians you know and form your group with them. That's the most comfortable route, but it won't meet the needs of people who don't know Christ. It's a good idea, though, to invite one or two Christian friends to form the nucleus of the study with you. As you do this, be aware that some believers feel they are called to be special "guardians of the truth." They can squelch discussion in your Bible study by insisting on clarifying every point and wanting to demonstrate their vast Bible knowledge. So be sure to share your vision of what this group will be, and enlist the prayer help of the Christian friends you invite.

Resist the temptation also to prejudge who might or might not be interested in Bible study. You'll be surprised by those who choose to come or not to come. The one you think is most secure may have the deepest hunger. If you're inviting neighbors, invite *everyone* within three or four blocks of your home. If you're beginning a Bible study at work, invite all of your colleagues. Open the invitation to all the members of your aerobics class, dorm floor, or bowling league. It's good to follow this pattern each time a study begins a new season, too. People who found reasons not to come last year may decide differently this year.

Before you invite anyone, you might want to do a "Jericho jog," either literally or mentally. Take a jog through your neighborhood, praying for each home as you go past. Or mentally "jog" through your office, praying for each potential group member. Pray that God will create a hunger for himself in your friends' hearts. Commit your outreach effort to him.

A simple invitation might say something like this:

---

*Come for dessert!*
*Place: 511 S. Maple St.*
*Time: 7:30 p.m.*
*After dessert, we'll discuss the possibility of forming a Bible study together. No need to be a religious expert!*
*Questions? Call 492-9645*

---

Of course "dessert" can be changed to pizza, coffee, or tacos, depending on your target group. You can either mail your invitations or deliver them personally to each person invited. Combining a verbal invitation and a written one is ideal. Notice that you aren't trying to "trick" people—you clearly state that the purpose of this get-together is to explore the possibility of a Bible study. It's important to be honest about your purpose from the start.

As your friends arrive, you may want to provide name tags. After enjoying refreshments together, pass out Bibles with bookmarks placed at the passage you will study. Don't assume that everyone will know how to locate a biblical reference. Stick with one passage, so no one will feel uncomfortable with unfamiliar Bible-hopping. You may even want to provide copies of the same

Bible version for everyone in the group. That way you can refer to page numbers that everyone can easily find.

Begin by explaining *your* reasons for being interested in a Bible study group: your desire to understand better what the Bible has to say for contemporary people in a troubled world, your need to be part of a group where you can get to know others better, and your need for encouragement to study the Bible regularly.

Lead a short sample study to give people an idea of what to expect from the study.[2] Sometimes it's helpful to have an outside friend come to your group to do this for you. You might say, "My friend Jack is part of a Bible study in his neighborhood, and he has agreed to lead a sample study for us to show us how this kind of study works." This approach puts you on the same level as the rest of the group and keeps you from being seen as the "expert."

If you use a studyguide, it's helpful for each person to have a copy of the sample study so that everyone can see exactly what's coming. (Most bookstores will let you buy a quantity of study-guides and return any you don't need.)

After a very short study, ask if anyone is interested in getting together regularly to continue this kind of study. Or, you might say, "This is how a Bible study works. Give it some thought, and we'll call to see if you'd like to try it."

It's best to begin with a six- or eight-week commitment, so that people don't feel like they are signing on forever. Decide on a time that is mutually convenient, and plan together to meet on that day.

### Your Target Group

How do you put together the right mix for your group? Some people insist that a group must be reasonably homogeneous in order to feel comfortable with each other and be able to focus on Bible study. If the needs of members are too different, much of the group's energy can go into creating relationships. And it might be difficult to find a common topic for study in a varied group.

On the other hand, educational theory suggests that diversity in a group is a positive force in the learning process. People develop and mature as they experience and resolve conflicts. So diversity can be desirable rather than detrimental. And the common topic is Jesus, whatever the needs may be.

Gladys Hunt describes one of the groups she started like this:

> No two of us were alike in background, in temperament, or in experience. Yet a miracle was going to take place. God was going to take the truth of one potent chapter recorded in the Bible and use it as a sword in each life to accomplish a specialized task in the individuals there.[3]

We have been in groups that resembled a cultural mosaic, with people from Australia, Japan, Germany, Nigeria, England, and the United States. Backgrounds in Bible knowledge were as varied as the nationalities represented. Surprisingly, these groups were very effective. Newcomers to Bible study brought an invigorating freshness to the discussion, and long-time Christians found excitement in being "on the cutting edge" of new discoveries in faith.

Observing the "ground rules" discussed in the last chapter will help keep a mixed group healthy. These three are especially important and bear repeating:

1. *Stick to the passage.* In a diverse group, usually it's best to start by studying a book of the Bible, rather than a topic. This helps to ensure that interpretations and applications are made in proper context.

2. *Avoid tangents.* Side issues may be interesting, but they are usually unproductive. Continually come back to the question, "What does the text say?"

3. *Let the Bible be the authority.* No one in the group should become the "answer person." Each answer should reflect what the

passage itself says. If it doesn't, graciously lead the group back to the text.

If your diverse group sticks to these guidelines, you can look forward to exciting growth together. All of us are needy people, regardless of where we are in our Christian journey. What a privilege to make our pilgrimage in the company of others through Bible study!

So be open to various mixes in your Bible studies. The variety is part of the excitement and wonder. It creates situations where only the Holy Spirit can receive the credit for the miracles that will take place. Even in so-called homogeneous groups, each group member will be unique and you will not lack for challenging relationships. If your group is diversified, make that diversity work for you, adding richness and new perspectives to your discussions.

**What to Study**

Usually outreach Bible studies are based on one of the Gospels, highlighting the person and work of Jesus. But the Holy Spirit can speak through virtually any part of the Bible. Some beginning groups find that Genesis is a great book for seekers. Don't hesitate to dip into books other than the Gospels if they hold a particular interest to your friends.[4]

Most groups find it helpful to use a studyguide. Forming good questions that encourage discussion is an art and takes a great deal of hard work. That work has already been done for you in some of the good studyguides available for beginning groups.[5]

Using studyguides has other advantages besides saving you a lot of work. When each member of the group has a copy of the same studyguide, there is no "secret leader's manual" to arouse suspicion. Also, leadership can be easily rotated among group members because the role of the leader becomes that of "question-asker" not "answer person." The Bible itself is the source of authority. And the Holy Spirit is the teacher.

He uses the experiences and insights of individual members to amplify truth. Studying in a group is a check on an individual's own understanding of the text. One person's commitment and honesty prods the reluctant heart of another.[6]

## Overcoming Hurdles

Maybe you're saying, "All of this sounds great, but I could never do it." That's because you're focusing on yourself instead of on God. He is already at work in your world—in you personally and in the lives of your acquaintances. After all, the idea of changing people through a personal encounter with Jesus is God's idea, not yours. So you can expect him to be with you each time you meet to study his Word.

It isn't enough just to focus on your own pilgrim journey. You need to point others to the King's Highway and help them interpret the Map to the Celestial City. Outreach Bible studies are a powerful means of bringing people to Christ. So open the door and let the Lion out of the cage. He'll defend himself!

### Questions for Reflection
1. What has been your experience in evangelism? What approaches have been effective? Which ones have been ineffective?

2. What are the obstacles that keep you from telling others about Christ? Could the approach of evangelistic Bible studies help you to overcome any of those hurdles?

3. Identify some people you know who are not believers in Jesus. Begin to pray for them regularly and start to make plans for inviting them to a Bible study.

**4.** If you don't know many non-Christians, what could you do to broaden your circle of friendships?

## Notes

**1.** Neighborhood Bible Studies, pioneered and directed by Marilyn Kunz and Kay Schell, is an organization devoted to outreach through small group studies. Their book, *How to Start a Neighborhood Bible Study*, gives practical help for those who want to reach out in this way. Much of the material in this chapter is based on their approach.

**2.** Details for a sample study are found in *How to Start a Neighborhood Bible Study*, available from Tyndale House Publishers, 338 E. Gundersen, Carol Stream, IL 60188.

**3.** Gladys Hunt, *You Can Start a Bible Study Group* (Wheaton, Ill.: Harold Shaw Publishers, 1984), p. 36.

**4.** See appendix for a sample study from John 3 which is very effective for beginning groups.

**5.** There are many excellent guides for evangelistic outreach studies. Among them are: *Meeting Jesus* by James Sire (Shaw Publishers); *Examining the Claims of Jesus* by Dee Brestin (Shaw Publishers); *Mark: God in Action* by Chuck and Winnie Christensen (Shaw Publishers); *Mark* by James Hoover (InterVarsity); *Mark: Examine the Record* by Marilyn Kunz and Catherine Schell (Tyndale); *Genesis: Walking with God* by Margaret Fromer and Sharrel Keyes (Shaw Publishers); *Great Passages of the Bible*, edited by Carol Plueddemann (Shaw Publishers); *Who Is Jesus? A Woman's Workshop on Mark* by Carolyn Nystrom (Zondervan); and *A Workshop on the Christian Faith* by Carolyn Nystrom (Zondervan).

**6.** Hunt, p. 36.

## *Why Small Groups Are Important to Me*

"All my life," said my neighbor between sips of coffee, "I've said I hope to go to heaven when I die. But this week I discovered that hoping isn't enough." We were meeting for a neighborly Bible study, and she'd learned in that week's lesson that she could be sure she was okay in God's eyes through faith in Christ's death for her sin. She was the first of several in that group of young mothers, all of them church-goers, who found eternal life in that small group Bible study. Through the years, I've found small groups to be a painfree way to share the good news of Jesus with others. The friendly atmosphere, the good feeling of being "in" with the group, the freedom simply to look at the Bible and discuss what it says and what it means—all of these make small groups wonderful birthing rooms for new Christians.

But it doesn't stop with new birth. Small groups also serve as nurseries and schools and even gymnasiums! It's in a small group that we care enough about one another to pray for and encourage our faltering baby steps. It's in a small group that we get feedback that corrects our misunderstanding of Scripture and reinforces our growth. And for most of my friends, it's been in a small group that they first dared to pray aloud, to lead a discussion, and to help another who was still struggling along the way.

Small groups help me stay on target. The accountability keeps me faithful in Bible study and prayer. And the interaction helps this task-oriented person remember that the Christian faith is relational.

Carol Wilson, Michigan

# 10
## World
## Pilgrims

*Involvement in this world should lead*
*to a deepening of our relationship with God,*
*and the deepening of this relationship should lead*
*to increasing involvement in the world.*
DAVID J. BOSCH, A Spirituality of the Road

As PILGRIMS, WE ARE ON A LIFELONG JOURNEY TOWARD OUR REAL Home. But in the meantime, we are in the world. The pilgrimage is not a mystical, individualistic journey in which the pilgrim is merely "fleeing from the contaminated world." Pilgrims cannot focus solely on their own salvation while letting the rest of the world go to hell.

If our pilgrimage is self-seeking, we disobey Jesus' command to be salt and light in the whole earth. We cannot be lone individualists. We must be world pilgrims, carrying out Jesus' Great Commission to make disciples in all nations. Pilgrims must care deeply both about the misery of people and the glory of God. God calls us out of the world, but he also sends us into the world. Pilgrims live and grow with this tension.

C.S. Lewis said, "A continual looking forward to the eternal world is not a form of escapism or wishful thinking, but one of the things a Christian is meant to do. It does not mean that we are to leave the present world as it is. If you read history, you will find that the Christians who did the most for the present world were just those who thought most of the next."[1]

## Small Groups and the Great Commission

As we travel through the world, we are called to make disciples of all nations (Matt. 28:18-20). Because we are citizens of heaven, we are not limited by national boundaries—the whole world is the parish of every pilgrim. Some pilgrims will travel intentionally to other cultures, but all pilgrims must demonstrate a deep concern for the world by keeping up to date on world affairs, by consistent prayer, and by sacrificial giving.

The needs of the world are greater now than they have ever been. More than three billion people have never received new life in Christ. This means that most of the people of the world do not have real life! Such a statement is not culturally arrogant. The Bible says: "God has given us eternal life, and this life is in his Son. He who has the Son has life; and he who does not have the Son of God does not have life" (1 John 5:11-12). We must catch a vision for the people of the world and love the world as Jesus loves it. Small groups are a natural means in many cultures for decision-making. Evangelistic outreach can be strengthened through the use of small groups.

The Great Commission is also a command to teach believers. About a billion people in the world are at least nominally Christian. But since pilgrims in every culture are traveling a difficult road, they desperately need the nurture that comes from being involved in a small group of caring Christians who are committed to studying and following the Map of the Word.

The decision-making process in rural societies is often guided by consensus, and traditional groups tend to emphasize conformity and cooperation rather than competition.[2] These values make small groups even more appropriate for evangelism and nurture in such societies.

Cross-cultural diversity is continuing to grow in America and in most urban centers of the world. Urban specialist Ray Bakke says,

> The United States really is becoming a third world country. For years the U.S. has been the largest Jewish nation. For years it has been the largest Irish nation. It is the second largest black nation in the world. (Only Nigeria of all the 53 countries of Africa has more black people than the United States.) Currently, only Mexico and Spain, maybe Argentina, have more Spanish people than the U.S. By the year 2000, Hispanics in the U.S. will out-number Anglos. Very soon Hispanics will out-number blacks.[3]

It's clear that more and more people can have a significant cross-cultural ministry without leaving home. Yet at the same time, racial and ethnic tensions are increasing. There is an urgent need for multi-cultural small groups that meet for fellowship, prayer, and Bible study. The world is coming to our neighborhoods, and the world will also be coming to small group Bible studies in those neighborhoods. Learning about cultural differences is essential for small group leaders who have the opportunity to be involved with several ethnic groups or sub-cultures.

Since all of us are called to be world pilgrims—whether we travel to another culture or other cultures come to us—it is important to understand the cultural values that influence small group behavior.

## The Universality of Small Groups

Small groups are not a recent North American fad. God created people as social beings with needs for interaction. Since people cannot survive in isolation, they must find ways to cooperate. The family of Adam and Eve was the first small group.

People in every culture belong to small groups that influence norms and require cooperation. In rural traditional societies, people often belong exclusively to family and extended family groups. Men and women in simpler societies interact almost continually in small groups with those they know intimately. In urban societies, people belong to different groups for work, play, hobbies, and religious activities. Groups in industrialized cultures are often less intimate, less all-encompassing, and more complex.[4] World-wide urbanization has led to new small group structures almost everywhere in the world. Small groups play an important role in all societies.

Several research studies suggest that urban and rural groups may operate with different dynamics. People anywhere in the world who live in rural sub-cultures tend to cooperate more willingly than people in urban sub-cultures.[5] Culture has an important influence on preferences for leadership styles. Some cultures prefer participatory leadership, while others prefer more autocratic and centralized styles of leadership.

Though small groups are found in every culture, group dynamics may differ widely from culture to culture. People who take part in cross-cultural groups need to expect differences and be able to adapt to cultural distinctives.[6]

## Cultural Values and Small Groups

We seldom think about our own cultural values. These values sink below the level of our awareness and we take them for granted. So when people from different cultures get together for a small group Bible study, there might be interpersonal friction without anyone knowing precisely why. Unnecessary misunderstandings can arise in cross-cultural small groups about leadership styles, conflict management techniques, and group goals. Confusion can even arise over the tone of voice or hand motion of another person in the group.

A person from one culture may think it impolite to begin the Bible study before everyone in the group arrives. Someone from another culture may think it rude to interrupt the study by coming late. Neither person sees the problem from the other's perspective. A recognition of basic cultural values in ourselves and in others can help cultivate greater love and patience within the group. We can learn to have a more effective ministry with people from different cultures who join small groups in our neighborhood or church.

While people are capable of using any cultural value for good or for evil, cultural values are not in themselves automatically moral values. In some cultures students show respect for their professor by looking at the floor when answering a question. In other cultures students show respect by interacting humorously with the professor. Neither approach is necessarily right or wrong. Yet cultural values *are* sinful if they contradict the universal and objective principles of Scripture. People cannot excuse sinful behavior by claiming it is "just the way they do it" in their culture. If a culture values treachery or greed, that value is in conflict with God's revealed principles of morality. We must avoid the extreme of narrow ethnocentrism as well as the other extreme of cultural relativism.

Various cultures, for example, may have different ways of "speaking the truth in love." In one culture a person may value the approach of a gracious but direct confrontation with a person who is causing a problem. In another culture, a person may value the approach of making suggestions through a mutual friend rather than through direct confrontation. Ethnocentrism makes it difficult to understand different perspectives of speaking the truth in love. On the other hand, a cultural relativist does not take seriously the universal ethical principles of both truth and love. Understanding cultural values helps to avert both of these errors.

Small group leaders who work with people of several cultures often look for a simple recipe of easy answers. Training in cross-cultural group dynamics becomes a long list of "dos" and "don'ts." Since each culture is different, and because there are major differences within each culture, such lists are almost worthless. The person working with people of other cultures needs to discern general principles and adapt these to changing situations. What are some of the significant cultural differences that affect cross-cultural groups?

## High-Context or Low-Context Basic Cultural Values

Probably the most fundamental difference between people's values is their degree of sensitivity to what is happening all around them. Some cultures encourage people to be very sensitive to the whole context around them, subtle though this may be. Other cultures teach people to be more deeply in touch with their own personal emotions and thoughts.

Edward T. Hall makes a helpful distinction between "high context" and "low context" cultures.[7] A high-context culture is made up of people who pay special attention to the concrete world around them. Everything in the physical setting communicates something significant: the atmosphere of the room, sounds, smells, expressions on people's faces, and body language. High-context people tend to remember people's names and details about events. The subtleties of the real-life setting intentionally communicate important information.

A low-context culture, on the other hand, is made up of people who pay special attention to ideas and abstract concepts. They may remember a conversation about an important topic but not remember the name of the person involved in the conversation. The specific words communicate more than the tone of voice used in making the statement. Low-context groups emphasize the details and analysis of ideas.

Some social scientists claim that Western values have been dominated by the thinking patterns of ancient Greece, which encouraged people to concentrate on ideas instead of events.[8] Thus Bible study groups in a Western society might be well able to analyze the ideas in a Bible passage, but be less in tune with the needs of the people in the group.[9]

No small group is totally low-context, focusing only on ideas, or totally high-context, focusing only on the present context. Small groups fall someplace in a continuum between very high and very low context. Groups that focus on abstract ideas might be classified as low-context; groups that tend primarily to the needs of the people around them would be more high-context. Small groups that emphasize a schedule regarding the number of verses to be studied and the amount of time to be spent on the study would tend toward the low-context end of the continuum. Groups that emphasize relationship-building without particular attention to schedule or agenda would tend toward the high-context end of the continuum.

Check out the characteristics of high- and low-context groups on the chart on the following pages.

### Implications for Small Group Leaders

A small group leader working with people of different cultures needs to know when to adapt his or her leadership style to the cultural preferences of the group and when to nudge the group to a more balanced perspective.

Low-context leaders in a high-context culture may need to be less "uptight" about starting and ending times. Lack of punctuality may be frustrating, but putting too much emphasis on schedules may build unnecessary resentment.

A missionary in Nairobi was initially perturbed with the women in her Bible study when they canceled a class in order to visit a woman in their group who had just given birth to a baby. After all, these women had signed a promise that they would attend all the sessions. But she was able to understand that the high-context Kenyan women were focusing on the needs of the new mother, while she, the low-context missionary, was focusing on the signed promise to attend classes. She wisely accepted the change in routine, realizing she could learn a great deal about caring relationships from the high-context women in her Bible study.

|  | **High-Context Small Group** | **Low-Context Small Group** |
|---|---|---|
| **Time** | Many things can happen at the same time. It may be difficult to begin and end on time, or isolate one activity at a time. | The group will begin and end on time. Events can be scheduled in an orderly sequence. People will want to stick to the passage. |
| **Communication Style** | Communication will be indirect, with emphasis on non-verbal messages. Tone of voice, posture, and facial features will have group meaning. | Communication will be direct, either spoken or written. The concept being discussed will be more important than the feelings behind the statement. |
| **Authority** | Prestige is given by the group and becomes almost permanent. Others will be expected to respect rank. Formal credentials are important and need to be evident. | Authority is earned by individual and personal effort. It is temporary and dependent on continued performance. Formal credentials are not as important as performance. |
| **Leadership Style** | Leadership is usually highly controlling in order to maintain group harmony and conformity. Leader often has charismatic personality. Leaders reward loyalty to the group. | Leaders will allow each person to have significant input into decision-making. Group members are more likely to question the ideas and decisions of the leader. Leaders respect individual initiative from group members. |
| **Conflict Resolution Style** | Indirect resolution is sought through mutual friends. Displeasure is shown through non-verbal, subtle communication. Conflict resolution may be avoided for as long as possible. | Resolution is sought through direct confrontation. People will meet face to face and explain the difficulty verbally. Speaking the truth will be emphasized. |

| | | |
|---|---|---|
| **Group Goals** | The purpose of the group will be to build interpersonal relationships. Group will be people-oriented. | The group will be task-oriented. Group will want to cover a specified number of verses or finish particular projects. |
| **Preferred Bible Passages** | Bible stories and history will be preferred. The Psalms and passages that encourage the imagination will also hold interest. | Bible doctrine from different parts of the Bible will be emphasized along with the didactic passages of the Epistles. |
| **Interaction Style** | High group cooperation and a tendency to conform to decisions of others will characterize style. Group harmony will be important. | Interaction will be personalized with an emphasis on individual "ownership" of ideas. Conformity will be de-emphasized. |
| **Religious Emphasis** | The Holy Spirit and the gifts of the Spirit will have special emphasis. Emotional commitment and a feeling of belonging is important. | A solid understanding of the Word of God and correct doctrinal belief is stressed. Expository sermons will be appreciated. |
| **Major Focus** | Testimonies and sharing of needs are emphasized. Application of biblical passages is important. | Bible study is the focus, with an emphasis on understanding and interpreting the major ideas of the passage. |
| **Difficulty** | Has problems relating life needs to the objective truth of the Bible. | Has difficulty relating objective truth of the Bible to the problems of life. |
| | Can lead to heresy. | Can lead to dead orthodoxy. |
| **Strengths** | Builds empathetic relationships. Christian commitment is fervent and caring. | Builds a solid understanding of God's truth. Places a healthy emphasis on personal ownership and responsibility. |

Leaders from low-context cultures should not be surprised when high-context members skip around between observation and application questions. It may seem to a low-context leader that the group members don't have the ability to stick to the point, when in actual fact they may see things more wholistically. Peter Chang explains the difference with this analogy: "In an American meal, one has steak, potatoes and peas placed separately on the plate; whereas in chop suey everything is mixed together. The latter is not without organization, but only organized differently."[10]

The imaginative or story sections of the Bible may be more appropriate for a high-context small group than a study from the Epistles. As a first study, a life-related topic such as the Christian Home may be more appropriate than a doctrinal study. High-context small groups may need encouragement to get into the Bible for actual study. A natural tendency may be to spend most of the time in sharing and testimonies, leaving little time for Bible study. Realize that discussion may be cut short when a member of the group with status makes a point. Others in the group may not wish to debate that person at the risk of hurting the harmony of the group. The credentials of the high-context leader will be important. In developing new leadership for the group, it might be better to cultivate an older person or someone with respected credentials.

On the other hand, high-context leaders working with low-context small groups will also need to be sensitive to cultural expectations. As leader, you may need to make an extra effort to be sure the group begins and ends on time. A study of Romans may be more appropriate than an applied topical study, at least initially. Evidence of your ability to lead will be more important than your charismatic personality or academic credentials. The high-context leader must not be offended when group members challenge his or her ideas, debate each other's ideas, or ignore non-verbal communication hints such as tone of voice or facial expressions. Low-context groups can disagree with each other's ideas and still be the best of friends.

Low-context group members can be nudged toward the strengths of the high-context setting. Encourage members to be more aware of nonverbal communication. Move beyond cerebral analysis to life-application. Encourage caring relationship-building. Adapt to cultural expectations but, where appropriate, borrow strengths from other settings as well.

There are strengths and weaknesses in both low-context and high-context groups. Small group interactions will vary in different cultural settings and even within one culture. Leaders will need to be flexible in matching group activities to the cultural style of the people in the group. When adapting small group Bible study materials to other cultures, it is not enough to adapt the language and the illustrations. Adaptations need to be made to the cultural values as well.[11]

Although an understanding of basic values is helpful, it's important to remember that people don't fit neatly into simple cultural categories. For example, it's too simplistic to assume that all Americans are individualistic and all Africans are collectivistic. There is a wide range of values in each culture. Even children within the same family may have very different values regarding time or goals. And people are also capable of changing their cultural values—"shifting gears" depending on the situation. An efficiency-oriented lawyer might become laid-back on vacation and be quite content to wait for fish to bite. But most people have preferred cultural values they feel comfortable with most of the time. These values are *preferences* rather than inborn characteristics—which means that when you are the leader of a small group Bible study, you can't stereotype people before you get to know them.

As the leader or member of a group, you can learn to appreciate different cultural values even if you don't feel fully at home with different ways of doing things. You can adapt to people with different cultural values, and those from other cultures can learn to adapt to practices they think odd.

Since conflicts over basic values can arise even within a culture, this kind of understanding is helpful for everyone. Husbands and wives from the same culture can unconsciously hold to different leadership values. Coworkers in an office, deacons in the same church, or neighbors in the same block can assume different basic values about goal setting.

World pilgrims face exciting challenges as they reach out to needy people in complex societies. Small groups can play an important role in cross-cultural ministry.

## Questions for Reflection

1. What examples have you seen of groups becoming "spiritually fat" while ignoring their responsibility for outreach?

2. Are the members of your small group "world pilgrims"? If not, how can you help them to develop a concern for the world?

3. What examples of cross-cultural diversity have you observed where you live? What possibilities do you see for outreach?

4. What cultural values influence the behavior of your small group? If you aren't sure, sharpen your observation skills and identify these values as you participate in your group.

5. How can you adapt your leadership style to the cultural preferences of your group? In what areas might you want to nudge your group toward more balanced perspectives?

## Notes

1. C.S. Lewis, *Mere Christianity* (London: Fontana Books, 1960), p. 116.
2. Leon Mann, "Cross-Cultural Studies of Small Groups" in *Handbook of Cross-Cultural Social Psychology*, Vol. 5., ed. Harry C. Triandis and Richard W. Brislin (Boston: Allyn and Bacon, 1980), pp. 167, 184. An interesting discussion of research on cross-cultural small groups.

**3.** Raymond J. Bakke, "The World of the 1990's: What Will Our Students Face?" in *F.Y.I.* (Washington D.C.: Christian College Coalition, Summer 1989).

**4.** Mann, pp. 155-209.

**5.** Ibid., p. 156.

**6.** For a thorough review of the literature relating to culture and communication, see William B. Gudykunst and Stella Ting-Toomey, *Culture and Interpersonal Communication* (Sage Publications, 2111 W. Hillcrest Dr., Newbury Park, CA 91320, 1988).

**7.** Edward T. Hall, *Beyond Culture* (Garden City, N.J.: Anchor Books, 1977), p. 91.

**8.** Ibid., p. 89.

**9.** For a fascinating discussion of inductive Bible study in another culture, see Peter S. C. Chang, "Steak, Potatoes, Peas and Chopsuey—Linear and Non-linear Thinking," in *Missions & Theological Education in World Perspective*, ed. Harvie M. Conn and Samuel F. Rowen (Associates of Urbanus; Box 457; Farmington, MI 48024, 1984), pp. 113-123.

**10.** Ibid., p.119.

**11.** See Marvin K. Mayers, *Christianity Confronts Culture*, for helpful insight about basic cultural values and how these influence cross-cultural ministry. Also see Jim and Carol Plueddemann, "Developing Curriculum in Another Culture" in *Interlit*, June, 1987, pp. 8-9.

*126*

## *Why Small Groups are Important to Us*

When we first went to Bolivia, we were encouraged to focus our ministry on the "new lost tribes" that were upwardly mobile, yet outsiders to the gospel. These decision-makers of Bolivian society are educated, creative, and self-sufficient. They are surrounded by a traditional religious system that fans their self-sufficiency and gives them a feeling of "divine right" to their position. Their tightly knit social structures tend to keep outsiders out.

What could God use to help break down the barriers to this virtually unreached group? How could we help meet some of the personal and family needs and get to the central spiritual vacuum? We found ourselves joining forces with what God had already started in this new area of outreach. Various women's Bible studies had been started, and several other couples' home Bible studies were in progress. A small church fellowship grew out of these Bible studies. It was from this fellowship that we found host families for the Salt and Light Family Living Exchange in which short-term workers help open doors of friendship by living in Bolivian homes. All of these ministries are beginning to bear fruit among the professional class. God has brought into existence two churches, a Christian Business Men's Committee, and a variety of new Bible study groups. These groups are inviting folks to a personal relationship with Jesus Christ and submission to his lordship. The dream of reaching Bolivia's decision-makers is becoming a reality.

Bob and Carol Givens, Bolivia

# 11

# Profiles of
# Pilgrim Groups

*The Christian life is not a solitary journey.*
*It is a pilgrimage made in the company of the committed.*
ROBERTA HESTENES, Using the Bible in Groups

SMALL GROUPS EXIST IN AN ALMOST UNLIMITED VARIETY OF EX-
pressions. Though many different terms are used to describe them,
the one unifying factor of the groups this book describes is their
common intent to organize into small, informal fellowships for the
purpose of growing in Christ. The groups we are talking about are
"growth groups" or "enabling groups." The focus is growing in
Christlikeness and obedience to God's purposes for pilgrims. A
wide variety of groups can accomplish this purpose.

## Study Groups

Bible study is the primary activity of a study group. But this doesn't
mean the group is limited to an academic, cerebral activity. Far
from it! The emphasis of discovery Bible study is dynamic interaction between life and the Word. We can never legitimately divide
Bible study and practice. An understanding of Bible truth is a call
to transformed living.

In addition to Bible study, time should be spent in the other basics of group life—prayer, fellowship, and outreach. These will grow naturally out of the group Bible study and will take different forms, depending on the nature of the group.

In an evangelistic Bible study, participants may not be comfortable with praying out loud. There are various ways to encourage prayer without putting people on the spot. As group members express needs, these can be written on small pieces of paper. At the end of the study, each person takes one request home and prays for that. Or, the group leader can mention each request out loud as the rest of the group prays silently for that need. Prayer and fellowship often become intertwined as group members share needs and commit these to God.

## Affinity Groups

These groups gather to strengthen relationships and to encourage members in their walk with God. The common denominator of these groups is a special interest, largely based on age, gender, geography, or employment. Such groups would include men's groups, women's groups, singles' groups, teen or college groups, senior citizens' groups, nurses' fellowships, office groups, airline attendants' groups, neighborhood groups, and many more.

*Time* magazine recently featured an article about prayer and Bible study groups attended by prominent political figures in Washington D.C.

> There are gatherings in the Capitol, State Department, Pentagon and White House, as well as special prayer meetings for lawyers, real estate agents, businessmen and journalists . . . At one time, the movement was male-oriented, but now there are sessions for couples and congressional wives.[1]

The distinctive pressures of Washington life bring people together in groups where they can experience support and growth among peers who have common needs and understandings.

Singles' groups would be another example of affinity groups. Single adults have a special and unique need for community and an ongoing sense of "family." Small groups can help to meet those needs and can provide settings for meaningful growth and outreach.

The possibilities for forming affinity groups are almost endless. The format of such groups can vary greatly, too. Many affinity groups choose to emphasize Bible study as the core of their activity. If so, they could also be called Bible study groups, with the distinctive of a special interest holding the group together. Prayer and fellowship grow naturally out of the common interests and needs of the group.

If you belong to an affinity group, consider being part of another group as well where you experience more diverse relationships. It's helpful and supportive to meet with others who are like you because you share similar interests and problems, but it's also healthy to be in a group with people who are different from you. Diversity can be enriching and growth-producing. If you are a single person, you might benefit from a group that includes some couples and a variety of ages. If you are a senior citizen, you might enjoy the perspective of younger people in your group, and your years of experience will add an important dimension to their learning as well.

## Support Groups

These groups offer help and encouragement for those with special needs. Examples include those who are unemployed or facing a career change, victims of abuse or co-dependency, those recovering from divorce, parents of adolescents, bereaved persons, blended families, eating-disorder personalities, and countless others.[2]

These groups recognize that brokenness can be a catalyst that God can use for wholeness and holiness.

It is important for those with serious needs to receive professional counseling. Such people should not depend on a support group for therapy. But informal support groups can contribute greatly to healing, especially when that healing comes from the Great Physician. Groups within the Christian community offer a dimension of help that no other environment can. Support groups that point wounded pilgrims to Christ offer ultimate help and care.

A grief-recovery group meets on Wheaton College's campus as a support for students who have lost a parent, sibling, or significant person in their lives. The group began in 1984, soon after Lyle and Mary Dorsett had moved to Wheaton from Colorado. Just months before their move, their ten-year-old daughter, Erika, had died very suddenly of meningitis. While working at the college library, Mary learned that her student assistant, Linda, had just lost her mother through a suicide death. Mary mourned with her and said, "Linda, you need a Mom and I need a daughter. Let's get together." From that small beginning, Mary soon realized that there were many more students on campus who were grieving significant losses. Like Mary, they had come to a community where no one knew their lost loved ones, and they had left their support systems at home. They desperately needed a strong support group on campus. Now there is an ongoing grief-recovery support group. Once a month, students gather at the Dorsett's home to talk about the grief process and to give prayer support to each other. It's an informal time, but specific topics are covered. Refreshments contribute to the comfortable setting. "It helps to have a styrofoam cup to play with while you talk about deep things," Mary explains.

Mary keeps track of anniversary dates when students will be having an especially hard time, remembering their loss with a note of personal encouragement. Besides the once-a-month group, students meet together for dinner at the cafeteria once a week. This is an unstructured time just for fellowship and support.

Mary points out that support groups like this one could have enormous outreach potential as well. On a secular campus, such a group would bring Christians and non-Christians together in a very natural way because of a common need. The same could be true of other kinds of support groups. Support groups can be powerful settings for ministry and outreach.

## Ministry Groups

Ministry groups focus on a particular task or outreach. Effective ministry groups recognize that the group task can also contribute to the development of individual members. Some group leaders see people simply as resources for accomplishing a job. But when leaders care about the growth of each group member as well as the accomplishment of the task, significant ministry happens in and through people.

There are many examples of groups that form for the purpose of outreach and ministry. The Church of the Saviour in Washington, D.C. is one of the best known. This is actually a cluster of six churches, and within each church are mission groups, each with a unique focus to meet particular needs. Church membership includes commitment to a mission group. Mission groups meet weekly for Bible study, prayer, personal sharing, and discussion of strategy and implementation of the group's mission. Group members are committed both to an "inward and outward journey."[3]

Ministry opportunities for small groups are unlimited. The goal is to meet people's needs spiritually, physically, emotionally, and socially. This could take the form of door-to-door witnessing, hospitality to international students, volunteering at a shelter for the homeless, or supporting a missionary. A small group may reach out simultaneously on various levels. Locally, group members might sponsor a refugee family or host an evangelistic Bible study. At the same time, they might actively support an inner-city ministry or correspond with a missionary in Paraguay. Even groups that are not primarily organized for ministry will find that times of outreach strengthen the life of the group and of individual members.

## Church Committees

Church committees are task groups that exist in every church, but often these committees don't see themselves as ministry groups. A committee is a ready-made small group. When committee members take time to care and grow together, their programs and responsibilities are strengthened and enhanced. They can minister to each other while they minister to others. Roberta Hestenes describes this as "moving committees into community."[4] Every committee should be a community, she says. Each committee should see itself as a ministry team, with members committed to each other as well as to the task. And the task is not just a job, but a ministry.

A church choir, then, is not just a group that provides special music to enhance congregational worship. Since members come together and spend time with each other every week, the choir has the potential to be a caring group that ministers to its members as well as to the church. This can happen as choir members pray together in twos or threes before practice begins or as they go on a weekend retreat together. Rather than detracting from the practice time, this kind of caring will enhance the choir's ministry. It will probably result in better music, too.

When people feel cared for, they are more productive. So beginning committee meetings with focused sharing and prayer can minister to members' needs and enhance the committee's task. If you're leading an evangelism committee, ask each person how he or she became a Christian. This kind of question will help members know each other better, and it can also give ideas for evangelism strategies. Or, take time to pray for the individual outreach efforts of each committee member. This will strengthen committee members and will remind them that they are a ministry team called to do evangelism and to enable others to do it. They aren't just a committee making decisions about evangelism strategies for the church, but are actively involved in evangelism themselves.

Seeing committees as small groups has significant ministry implications. As members work together, they care for each other. The task helps to develop pilgrims, and ministry is enhanced as well.

## Family Groups

Sociologically and anthropologically, the family is considered the most basic small group. We should not overlook its potential for enhancing spiritual growth and for ministry. All of the elements that go into making any small group a healthy one can also apply to the family. The family is a natural small group where members can learn to love each other, pray together, study the Bible together, and minister together. If any of these elements are missing, the potential of the family group is minimized. By nature, families are intergenerational. This feature creates unique challenges and potential. Intergenerational learning can enhance growth as family members at different stages of life learn from each other. It's also a challenge to maximize the intergenerational potential without getting bogged down by the differences each age represents.[5]

Psalm 145 describes the beauty of one generation telling another about God's mighty acts. Deuteronomy 6 instructs parents to impress their children with God's commands through verbal and symbolic activities that will be memorable and convincing. Psalm 78 also emphasizes the responsibility of each generation to tell the next generation the praiseworthy deeds of the Lord. Families can benefit by recognizing their potential as small groups and by intentionally maximizing that potential through healthy small group practices.

## Teen Groups

Good things happen when teenagers meet in small groups. Youth workers who use small groups to complement large group activities report tremendous benefits.

After twelve years of youth leadership, teen leaders Jeff and Ramona Tucker are convinced of the benefits of small groups. When fifteen-year-old Trisha first came to "Group" (a Bible study), she was incredibly shy. After several months of support from the teens in her small group, she began to trust them. First she shared how she felt about school; eventually Trisha risked opening up to her group about her family. They surrounded her with a love that didn't change when they learned the history of sexual abuse in Trisha's home. For the first time, Trisha really felt loved. And not long ago, Trisha led her "Group" in a study on love and forgiveness!

Smaller groups provide settings where a variety of maturity levels can be ministered to more effectively. While the group as a whole may not get past short, topical Bible studies, smaller groups can focus on in-depth book studies. These smaller studies are excellent places to develop leadership among teens as they learn to study Scripture for themselves and to lead others. Small group Bible studies provide the kind of interaction that enhances growth in camp settings, catechism or confirmation classes, and school outreach ministries.

## Sunday School Classes

Sunday school classes don't automatically qualify as small groups, but they have that potential. Just gathering each Sunday in the same room to study a lesson falls short of what's needed for a healthy small group. But if the class intentionally meets individual needs through interactive Bible study, fellowship, and prayer, it can become a powerful small group. To do this, the class needs to stay small enough to provide individual care. If the class gets large, it can still break up into smaller care groups. The ministry of Sunday school can be greatly enhanced when classes see themselves as small group settings where aims and methods take into account the nature of pilgrim learners and help them toward Christlikeness.

## House Churches

Unlike most of the small groups we have described in this book, the house church is independent and self-contained. It is an "intentional Christian community" to which members are expected to invest large amounts of time, energy, and resources. Members generally do not attend other churches, seeing their primary, if not exclusive, commitment to the house church. Unlike most informal small groups, house churches emphasize worship and financial giving along with the other aspects of small group life. The intensity of commitment can lead to strong rewards in terms of growth and community, but it is not without its difficulties. Though the house church movement is beyond the scope of this book, there are many excellent resources that describe it well.[6]

Jesus promised that "where two or three come together in my name, I am there with them." Many different kinds of small groups help to strengthen and encourage pilgrims in their adventure of faith. It's important to remember that small groups are not ends in themselves, but means toward the goal of becoming like Christ and giving glory to God.

## Questions for Reflection
**1.** What type of small group would minister best to the needs around you? Are there possibilities for small group ministry that you haven't considered before?

**2.** Do you lead a committee whose ministry would be enhanced if you approached it as a small group? What steps can you take to help your committee see itself as a ministry team? How can you use your committee's task to develop individual team members?

**3.** How can you maximize your family's potential as a healthy small group?

**4.** Would you say that your Sunday school class qualifies as a small group? If not, how could it be structured to function as a healthy small group?

**Notes**

**1.** Richard N. Ostling, "Inside the Bible Beltway," *Time*, February 6, 1989, p. 56.

**2.** Stephen Ministries trains lay people for caring ministries in the church. For resources, write to Stephen Ministries, 1325 Boland, St. Louis, MO 63117 (314-645-5511).

**3.** The ministries of The Church of the Saviour are described in Elizabeth O'Connor's books, *Call to Commitment* and *Journey Inward, Journey Outward*. The founding pastor, Gordon Cosby, has written *Handbook for Mission Groups*. These books are available from Potter's House, 1658 Columbia Road, N.W., Washington, DC 20009.

**4.** Roberta Hestenes, *Building Christian Community through Small Groups*, video and audio cassette tape, Fuller Seminary Media Services, Fuller Seminary, Pasadena, CA 91182 (818-584-5227).

**5.** See Patricia Griggs, *Generations Learning Together* (Nashville: Abingdon, 1976).

**6.** See C. Kirk Hadaway, Stuart A. Wright, and Francis M. DuBose, *Home Cell Groups and House Churches* (Nashville: Broadman Press, 1987).

## *Why Small Groups Are Important to Me*

For fifteen years going to Bible study was like going to work. I attended four small groups a week. I wrote the schedules, arranged for leaders, searched for baby-sitters, made suggestions to hostesses, supplied choices of curriculum, followed up newcomers, researched knotty theological issues, counseled people with personal problems, and planned group holiday celebrations. Because I write inductive Bible studies for a living, these four groups were my laboratory, the place where I worked. Sure everybody else pitched in and helped. But they helped *me*—I carried the primary burden.

Good things happened. People got excited about studying Scripture. They grew closer to God. They found local churches and joined them. They learned to pray for each other—and to thank God for answered prayer. They began to teach their children to love God. I grew too.

Then came the year that a car accident killed our oldest daughter, pregnant with our first grandchild. A short time later, our oldest son was hospitalized because of a mental breakdown. At first, I decided to drop out of all my small groups. After all, I couldn't predict my emotional condition, or whether I would have to make a quick trip to the hospital. I didn't feel like an authority on anything that required faith. And I certainly didn't want responsibility for someone else's faith.

But I changed my mind. Instead, I made adjustments. I dropped, into other capable hands, a small group Sunday school class that required a lot of preparation. I moved out of a small church group that had served me well for many years because of its stimulating academic challenge. For that year, I substituted a group that emphasized worship and personal ministry. But I stayed with my neighborhood groups, the groups where I worked. Or, rather, they stayed with me. Other people arranged schedules. Leaders, hostesses, sitters emerged. For years I had taught that groups need to become self-sufficient, not dependent on any one person. Now I experienced it.

The people from these small groups who had cared for our family the week of Sheri's death—with food, housing, transportation, hugs, and tears—now took over the Bible studies. And they ministered to me. Sometimes I just sat. Sometimes I cried. Sometimes I told the same stories about Sheri over and over. They listened and cared and prayed. And God's work went on.

It wasn't easy for me or them. Sometimes I thought if I had to listen to one more minute of normal cheery conversation I would bolt for the door. (I didn't. But I warned them that I might.) Sometimes they just held me—like the time I came straight to an evening group after an hour of tearfully making my way through the grocery store with Sheri's favorite foods leaping off the shelves at me with every turn of my cart.

I knew I was beginning to recover when a song sheet from one of the groups caught my eye from its discard spot on the dining-room table. For the first time in weeks, I felt like singing praise—a little. The first time I lead a group again, I prepared with all the nervousness of a novice. During the study I could feel others in the group helping guide the discussion as if I were a first-time leader, and I appreciated their care. As the year wore on, we all gained insight into suffering, theirs and mine. And we grew in our trust of a God who, for reasons known only to himself, does not protect us from pain but instead enters into suffering with us.

I'm glad I stayed with my small groups that year. I learned what it is like to receive ministry: a little embarrassing, a little humbling, a lot out of control. (I no longer ask why it is that people who receive help from a group during a crisis in their lives often leave that group when they have recovered to "normal." But I do not plan to follow that pattern myself.) The year that I stayed with my groups gave me increased respect for God's ability to work in spite of human weakness, to work through the avenues of human love, and to redeem what is awful—thereby bringing glory to himself.

Carolyn Nystrom, Illinois

# 12
# Strengthening Pilgrim Groups

*'Tis Jesus the First and the Last,*
*Whose Spirit shall guide us safe home;*
*We'll praise Him for all that is past,*
*And trust Him for all that's to come.*
JOSEPH HART

As WE PRESS ON IN THE JOURNEY, WE LONG FOR THE DAY WHEN our ultimate purpose will be fulfilled and "we shall be like him, for we shall see him as he is." The sure hope of that joy and the encouragement of faithful pilgrims spurs us on.

Meanwhile, because pilgrims are far from perfect, there is no such thing as a perfect growth group. Building small groups is difficult. But weak groups can become stronger, and healthy groups can grow even more vigorous. No matter how discouraging or how successful the group, there is always the exciting expectation for improvement.

My grandfather used to announce repeatedly that "anything worth doing was worth doing *well*." The proverb frightened me away from trying new things. I felt that if I couldn't do something right I shouldn't try it at all. But the opposite is true! As G.K. Chesterton said, "If a thing is worth doing, it is worth doing badly"—*at first*. Small groups are very much worth doing, but they are difficult to do well. Small group leaders shouldn't be discouraged with less-than-perfect experiences. The wise small group leader is not the person who succeeds the first time, but the person who knows how to learn from experience. Too many small groups stagnate and die because leaders aren't learning to build stronger groups.

## The Spiritual Battle

There will never be a guaranteed, "leader-proof" technology for small groups, but we *can* learn how to learn from experience. We will never be in full control of all the things that help or hinder small groups. Forces beyond our comprehension influence the group process. Pilgrims are involved in a struggle between supernatural forces of good and evil. No matter how skilled leaders may be, group process skills will never overcome the problem of evil. When people are determined to rebel against God, the best small group leader or curriculum will be ineffective. It is impossible for groups to have a life-changing influence on people without the power of the Holy Spirit.

A powerful way to improve small groups is through prayer. We have supernatural resources available to us: The Holy Spirit is at work through the Word and through spiritually gifted Christians. When preparing to lead a group, it makes good sense to pray for each person in the group, to pray through the agenda of the meeting, and to pray through each Bible verse to be studied.

But just because leaders are not in control of the most important ingredients in small groups (the spiritual factors) does not mean they should be satisfied with weak, anemic groups. Though we will never fully understand the group process, God has given us significant responsibility in it. The parable of the growing seed in Mark 4 illustrates the point (verses 26-29). The farmer is required to do the hard work of planting the seed. He is given wisdom to know when to pull weeds and skill to harvest the crop. But the farmer is not expected to understand the growth process fully. "Whether he sleeps or gets up, the seed sprouts and grows, though he does not know how. All by itself the soil produces grain . . ." (Mark 4:27-28). Though the farmer isn't in control of all the aspects of producing a crop, he is responsible to do his part faithfully.

In the same way, though the small group leader is not in control of all the influences that strengthen or weaken a group, he or she is called to do the best possible job of leading. Group leaders have responsibilities to strengthen and improve the effectiveness of small groups even though God is ultimately in charge of the process.

When planning for a small group, we intuitively think about three rather common-sense elements—group context, group activities, and group outcomes. When we think about *strengthening* or evaluating a small group, we can think about these same three elements.[1]

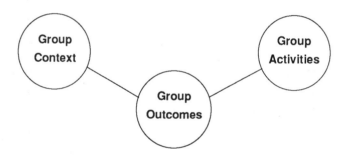

## The Group Context

What is the small group's present *context*? Important questions to ask about context include: What are the expectations of the people in the group? Do they expect to study the Bible? Do they expect to spend a significant amount of time in prayer or outreach? Do people in the group have previous experience with Bible studies? Does the leader have previous experience? Do group members have special needs? Is there a need for baby-sitters? Is the physical setting comfortable? How much time is available? Is there enough time for informal visiting and refreshments? These are only examples of the dozens of questions one could ask about context.

Often the simplest way to improve the quality of a small group is to anticipate the context better. Perhaps there is not enough time for prayer because people take longer than anticipated with refreshments. You could improve the group by serving refreshments at the end of the study or by beginning a little earlier.

## Group Activities

What kinds of small group *activities* do you plan? Will you spend most of your time studying the Bible? What part of the Bible will you study—a book of the Bible or a topic? Will you use a studyguide? What other activities will you include—singing, prayer, refreshments? Are you planning social times? Will you include outreach tasks in your group such as supporting missionaries or planning an evangelistic strategy?

One good way to strengthen your small group is to better match the activities with your context. If people expect a committee-type task group, they may be surprised to find so much time spent in prayer. It's important to let people know what kind of group you intend. Maybe there is a mis-match between the kind of people in the group and the activities. If people in the group are new to Bible study, it may not be a good idea to begin with a topical Bible study that assumes people can quickly find verses in many parts of the Bible.

It is important to match the activities of the group with the context of members' needs, interests, and abilities.

## Group Outcomes

What kinds of results would you like to see in the lives of group members? Are they seeking help with specific problems in their lives? Would they like to have a better understanding of the basic themes of Scripture? Do they want to learn to trust the Lord more fully? Some groups have an evangelistic purpose, others seek to teach people how to pray or study the Bible. The purpose of other groups is worship. One way to strengthen your small group is to take time to discuss the purposes of the group and to see how these match up with the context and the activities.

**A Model for Evaluation**

Healthy groups have a consistent relationship between their context, activities, and outcomes. One of the best ways to strengthen your group is to look for ways to make the relationship between these three factors more consistent. Groups will have trouble if the outcomes don't match the context of the group, and outcomes will seldom be accomplished if group activities don't relate to the purposes. The best way to evaluate a group is to work at making these three factors more consistent with each other. The following model is a helpful tool for evaluation:[2]

|  | **The Plan**<br>What was your<br>plan for the group? | **The Actual**<br>What actually happened in the group? |
|---|---|---|
| **Small Group Context** |  |  |
| **Small Group Activities** |  |  |
| **Small Group Outcomes** |  |  |

The purpose for evaluating a group is to strengthen it. When you compare the *intended plan* with the *actual result* you can find reasons for the differences and make adjustments accordingly. (Sometimes the actual result will be even better than intended!)

Leaders tend to evaluate groups at the end of the year. Think instead in terms of making your small group better each time you meet. How much better to use evaluation as an on-going process that can strengthen groups on a continual basis from week to week. Anything worth doing well is worth doing better. This evaluation model has been used effectively to evaluate a broad range of ministry activities, from Sunday school curriculum to mission board strategies. It can also be a great help for evaluating and strengthening small group ministry settings.

## An Example

Suppose you plan an evangelistic Bible study outreach. The *context* you plan for includes non-Christian neighbors who will meet for a four-week Lenten series on Thursday evenings from 7:30 to 9:00 P.M. in your home. The *activities* you plan include a topical study of 'The Cross" (from Bibles you will provide), prayer, and singing. The intended *outcomes* you hope for include getting to know your neighbors better, an increased interest in Bible study, and the conversion of those who do not have a personal relationship with Christ.

The *actual context* is much as you anticipated, but one couple was not able to come because they couldn't find a babysitter. In talking with them, you find that they would be willing to have the group meet at their home so they can attend and still be with their children. So the location of the next study is changed to their home. As you evaluate the *activities* you conclude that the topical study was difficult because group members weren't familiar with the location of the books of the Bible. You decide that for the remaining three studies, you will stick to one passage each time, using Bibles with bookmarks. The singing proved awkward, since people weren't familiar with the same songs, so you decide not to include this for the other sessions. Prayer was also difficult, since most of the group members were not used to praying out loud. For future sessions, you plan to close with a simple prayer, encouraging each person to pray silently. The actual *outcomes* are harder to observe, but after the first evening, you observe that neighbors enjoyed getting to know each other better. To facilitate this even more, you begin to think about having an Easter breakfast for everyone in the group. You continue to pray that group members will be eager to study the Bible and that some will come to know Christ. Realizing how important this is, you ask some of your Christian friends to pray with you about the remaining studies. So by comparing the *intended* context, activities, and outcomes with the *actual* context, activities, and outcomes, you can strengthen the effectiveness of your outreach in the remaining sessions. The foundational criterion for evaluating a small group is whether or not it helps people to know and love God.

### The End of the Pilgrimage

Pilgrim groups give encouragement and strength to help us persevere in the journey of faith and to bring others to the Path. And so we look forward to the day when faith will be made sight and we will praise God forever in eternal delight. The Celestial City is the end of the pilgrimage, not only because pilgrims can rest from the perils of the journey, but because they will no longer be hindered in their knowledge and praise of God. We look forward with unimaginable anticipation to that goal, because we shall be like him when we see him face to face (1 John 3:2). Our goal as pilgrims is not merely to arrive at the heavenly city, but to face the King of Kings and Lord of Lords singing, "Hallelujah! Salvation and glory and power belong to our God. . . . Hallelujah! For our Lord God Almighty reigns. Let us rejoice and be glad and give him glory!" (Rev. 19:1, 6-7).

**Questions for Reflection**
1. Think carefully about your small group. Do you recognize the spiritual struggle in which you are involved or do you tend to think of your problems primarily in terms of "group dynamics"? Without minimizing the need for understanding group process skills, pray continually for each of your group members and the spiritual battle each one faces.

2. How often do you evaluate the effectiveness of your group? How could continual evaluation strengthen your group?

3. How can evaluation help your group to focus on its ultimate purpose?

4. How would you evaluate your individual growth toward Christlikeness? Pray for a clear vision of what God wants for you and your group.

**Notes**
1. This model is adapted from a curriculum evaluation model by Robert Stake, "The Countenance of Educational Evaluation," *Teacher's College Record* (Vol. 68, 1967), pp. 523-540.
2. Ibid.

✦✦✦✦✦✦✦✦✦✦✦✦✦✦✦✦✦✦✦✦✦✦✦✦

love one another
serve one another
bear with one another
be devoted to one another
encourage one another
build each other up
accept one another
do not slander one another
instruct one another
admonish one another
carry each other's burdens
be kind and compassionate to one another
forgive each other
speak to one another with psalms, hymns, and spiritual songs
submit to one another
do not lie to each other
spur one another on to love and good deeds
confess your sins to each other
pray for each other
clothe yourselves with humility toward one another
greet one another
be at peace with each other
comfort one another

John 13:34; Galatians 5:13; Ephesians 4:2; Romans 12:10; Hebrews 10:25; 1 Thessalonians 5:11; Romans 15:7; James 4:11; Romans 15:14; Colossians 3:16; Galatians 6:2; Ephesians 4:32; 5:19; 5:21; Colossians 3:9; Hebrews 10:24; James 5:16; 1 Peter 5:5; 5:14; Philippians 2:3; Mark 9:50; 1 Thessalonians 4:18 (KJV)

✦✦✦✦✦✦✦✦✦✦✦✦✦✦✦✦✦✦✦✦✦✦✦✦

# Appendix

Sample Discovery Bible Study*

## Comforted to Comfort
## 2 Corinthians 1:1-11

One of the most difficult kinds of letters to write is a "sympathy note." Have you noticed that the most comforting notes are often written by those who have had firsthand experience with sorrow themselves?

In this letter, Paul writes to suffering people from the perspective of one who has also suffered. In fact, Paul sees a direct correlation between his suffering and the comfort he offers.

**1.** Describe a time when you were comforted by someone or a time when you were a means of comfort to another person.

**2. Read 1 Corinthians 1:1-11.** What authority does Paul claim as he writes this letter?

**3.** In what ways are "grace and peace" (verse 2) a summary of the Good News and of ultimate comfort?

**4.** How does Paul's description of God (verse 3) help you to understand his nature?

**5.** What principles about suffering and comfort can you learn from verses 4-7? What practical examples of these principles have you experienced?

**6.** How does Paul's description of his suffering make you feel (verses 8-11)?

**7.** What had Paul learned about himself through his suffering? About God?

**8.** What confidence does Paul affirm (verse 10)?

**9.** What help does Paul need from the Corinthians? What will be the result of this help?

**10.** Can you think of a time when God helped you not only to endure suffering but also to experience benefits from it?

**11.** Where are you right now in terms of comfort—are you experiencing comfort, giving comfort, or in need of comfort? What does this passage suggest for your needs?

**12.** Pray together, asking God to help you set your hope on him (verse 10) and to make your life a comfort to someone who is suffering. Identify individuals within your group or outside of it who need your prayers for comfort or deliverance (verses 10-11).

*From 2 *Corinthians: Strengthened by Struggle*, a Fisherman Bible Study-guide by Jim and Carol Plueddemann.

Sample Outreach Bible Study*

## A New Birth
## John 3:1-21

When reporters questioned presidential candidate Jimmy Carter about his religious beliefs, he answered, "I have been born again." And suddenly this rather strange term made headlines everywhere. Some politicians claimed it, others ranted against it, comedians made fun of it.

But in spite of all the publicity, most people still didn't know what *born again* meant. "Mega-religious," "holy-roller," "Bible-banger" and just plain "weird" all got thrown into the same word pile. Before long, people who knew they were born again felt embarrassed to say so. Nobody knew what they were talking about anyway.

In spite of surprised newscasters, *born again* is not really a new term. Jesus himself used it centuries ago in a private conversation with a Jewish religious leader named Nicodemus.

**1.** What feelings does the phrase "born again" bring to your mind?

**2. Read John 3:1-3.** What steps had Nicodemus already taken that would prepare him to receive what Jesus said?

**3.** What reasons did Nicodemus have to be surprised at Christ's response to him?

**4.** Read John 3:3-15. What phrases here show that being born again is important?

**5.** What patterns from nature did Jesus use to help Nicodemus understand? What spiritual truths do these natural happenings illustrate?

**6. Look up Numbers 21:6-9.** How might this incident in Jewish history help Nicodemus understand Christ and his message?

**7.** If you were Nicodemus, what further questions would you want to ask Jesus at this point?

**8. Read John 3:16-21.** Look carefully at John 3:16. Many theologians call this verse "the Christian message in a nutshell." What can you know about Christianity from this verse? Think about the meaning of each word or phrase.

**9.** According to this paragraph (verses 16-21), does a person start out right or wrong with God? Why?

**10.** In what two ways can a person respond to Jesus? What is the result of each of these two responses?

**11.** What reasons did Jesus give for why a person might not choose to believe in him?

**12.** Verse 19 suggests that one reason people choose not to believe in Jesus is that "Men loved darkness." What is comfortable about physical darkness? Why might similar attractions cause people to enjoy spiritual darkness?

**13.** People sometimes criticize Christianity as a "one-way gospel." What phrases from today's passage suggest that there is, in fact, only one way to God?

**14.** If what Jesus says in John 3 is "the truth," how must a person come into a right relationship with God?

**15.** Do you think that "born again" is still a good term for someone who has lived in spiritual darkness and now experiences a right relationship with God? Why or why not? Why might this new relationship with God seem like new birth to someone who has lived in spiritual darkness?

*From *Great Passages of the Bible*, a Fisherman Bible Studyguide edited by Carol Plueddemann. This study was written by Carolyn Nystrom.

# Bibliography and Resources

## Books and Resources about Small Groups

Cho, Paul Yonggi. *Successful Home Cell Groups.* Plainfield, N.J.: Bridge Publishing, 1981.

Davies, James A. "Small Groups: Are They Really So New?" *Christian Education Journal,* Volume V, Number 2. Glen Ellyn, Ill.: Scripture Press, Fall, 1984.

Dibbert, Michael T. and Frank B. Wichern. *Growth Groups: A Key to Christian Fellowship and Spiritual Maturity in the Church.* Grand Rapids: Zondervan, 1985.

Durnbaugh, Donald F. "Intentional Community in Historical Perspective" in *The House Church Evolving.* Arthur Foster, ed. Chicago: Exploration Press, 1976.

Hadaway, C. Kirk, Stuart A. Wright, and Francis M. Dubose. *Home Cell Groups and House Churches.* Nashville: Broadman Press, 1987.

Hestenes, Roberta. *Using the Bible in Groups.* Philadelphia: Westminster Press, 1985.

——————. *Building Christian Community through Small Groups,* video and audio cassette tape, Fuller Seminary Media Services, Fuller Seminary, Pasadena, CA 91182 (818-584-5227).

Nicholas, Ron, et al. *Good Things Come in Small Groups: The Dynamics of Good Group Life.* Downers Grove, Ill.: InterVarsity Press, 1985.

Olsen, Charles M. *Cultivating Religious Growth Groups.* Philadelphia: Westminster Press, 1984.

## Books for Small Group Leaders

Coleman, Lyman. *Training Manual for Small Group Leaders.* Littleton, Co.: Serendipity House, 1987.

Cosby, Gordon. *Handbook for Mission Groups.* Potter's House, 1658 Columbia Rd., N.W., Washington, DC 20009. (Reprint available from Fuller Seminary Bookstore, Pasadena, CA 91182.)

Gibb, Jack R. "Dynamics of Educational Leadership" in William R. Lassey and Marshall Sashkin, *Leadership and Social Change,* third edition. San Diego: University Associates, 1983.

Griffin, Em. *Getting Together: A Guide for Good Groups.* Downers Grove, Ill.: InterVarsity Press, 1982.

Keyes, Sharrel. *Working Out Together: Keeping Your Group in Shape.* Wheaton, Ill.: Harold Shaw Publishers, 1985.

Navigators. *How to Lead Small Group Bible Studies.* Colorado Springs: NavPress, 1987.

Nicholas, Ron, et al. *Small Group Leader's Handbook.* Downers Grove, Ill.: InterVarsity Press, 1982.

Nyquist, James, and Jack Kuhatschek. *Leading Bible Discussions.* Downers Grove, Ill.: InterVarsity Press, 1985.

Richards, Lawrence, O. *99 Ways to Start a Study Group and Keep It Growing.* Grand Rapids.: Zondervan Publishing Co., 1987.

Stewart, Ed and Nina Fishwick. *Group Talk!* Ventura, Calif.: Regal Books, 1986.

Wald, Oletta. *The Joy of Discovery in Bible Study.* Minneapolis: Augsburg, 1975.

_____. *The Joy of Teaching Discovery Bible Study.* Minneapolis: Augsburg, 1976.

Ward, Ted. "Servants, Leaders and Tyrants" in *Missions and Theological Education in World Perspective,* Harvie M. Conn and Samuel F. Rowen, eds. Farmington, Mich.: Associates of Urbanus, 1984.

## Books about Outreach Bible Studies

Brestin, Dee. *Finders Keepers: Introducing Your Friends to Christ and Helping Them Grow.* Wheaton, Ill.: Harold Shaw Publishers, 1983.

Jacks, Bob, Betty Jacks, and Ron Wormser, Sr. *Your Home A Lighthouse: Hosting an Evangelistic Bible Study.* Colorado Springs: NavPress, 1986.

Kunz, Marilyn and Catherine Schell. *How to Start a Neighborhood Bible Study.* Wheaton, Ill.: Tyndale, 1981.

Hunt, Gladys. *You Can Start a Bible Study Group.* Wheaton, Ill.: Harold Shaw Publishers, 1984.

Lum, Ada. *How to Begin an Evangelistic Bible Study.* Downers Grove, Ill.: InterVarsity Press, 1971.

Peace, Richard. *Small Group Evangelism: A Training Program for Reaching Out with the Gospel.* Downers Grove, Ill.: InterVarsity Press, 1985

## Books on Related Topics

Bellah, Robert N., Richard Madsen, William M. Sullivan, Ann Swidler, and Steven M. Tipton. *Habits of the Heart: Individualism and Commitment in American Life.* New York: Harper and Row, 1986. A sociological study of American culture.

Bonhoeffer, Dietrich. *Life Together.* New York: Harper and Row, 1969.

Groome, Thomas. *Christian Religious Education.* San Francisco: Harper and Row, 1980.

LeBar, Lois E. and James E. Plueddemann. *Education That Is Christian.* Wheaton, Ill.: Victor Books, 1989, revised edition.

O'Connor, Elizabeth. *Call to Commitment.* New York: Harper and Row, 1976.

Snyder, Howard A. *The Problem of Wine Skins: Church Structure in a Technological Age.* Downers Grove, Ill.: InterVarsity Press, 1979.

———. *The Radical Wesley and Patterns for Church Renewal.* Downers Grove, Ill.: InterVarsity Press, 1980.

Traina, Robert A. *Methodical Bible Study.* Grand Rapids, Mich.: Zondervan, 1985.

## Books on Small Groups from a Secular Perspective

Beebe, Steven A. and John T. Masterson. *Communicating in Small Groups: Principles and Practices.* Glenview, Ill.: Scott, Foresman and Co., 1982.

Bormann, Ernest G. and Nancy C. Bormann. *Effective Small Group Communication.* Minneapolis: Burgess, 1980.

Bradford, Leland P., ed. *Group Development.* San Diego, Calif.: University Associates, 1978.

_____. *Making Meetings Work: A Guide for Leaders and Group Members.* San Diego, Calif.: University Associates, 1976.

Cathcart, Robert S. and Larry S. Samovar. *Small Group Communication: A Reader,* fourth edition. Dubuque, Iowa: Wm. C. Brown, 1984.

Johnson, David W. and Frank P. Johnson. *Joining Together: Group Theory and Group Skills.* Englewood Cliffs, N.J.: Prentice-Hall, 1982, second edition.

Kirschenbaum, Howard and Barbara Glaser. *Developing Support Groups.* La Jolla, Calif.: University Associates, 1978.

## Books to Aid Cross-cultural Ministry

Chang, Peter S.C. "Steak, Potatoes, Peas and Chopsuey—Linear and Non-linear Thinking" in *Missions and Theological Education in World Perspective,* Harvie M. Conn and Samuel F. Rowen, eds. Farmington, Mich.: Associates of Urbanus, 1984.

Gudykunst, William B. and Stella Ting-Toomey. *Culture and Interpersonal Communication.* Newbury Park, Calif.: Sage Publications, 1988.

Hall, Edward T. *Beyond Culture.* Garden City, N.J.: Anchor Books, 1977.

Johnstone, Patrick. *Operation World* (William Carey Library, P.O. Box 128-C, Pasadena, CA 91104).

Mann, Leon. "Cross-Cultural Studies of Small Groups" in *Handbook of Cross-Cultural Social Psychology,* Vol 5., Harry C. Triandis and Richard W. Brislin, eds. Boston: Allyn and Bacon, 1980.

Mayers, Marvin K. *Christianity Confronts Culture: A Strategy for Cross-Cultural Evangelism.* Grand Rapids: Zondervan, 1977.

Plueddemann, Jim and Carol. "Developing Curriculum in Another Culture" in *Interlit,* June, 1987.

Reapsome, Martha. "People Can Unravel the Bible—If We Let Them" in *Evangelical Missions Quarterly,* Vol. 19, No. 3, July 1983.

## Resources for Group Bible Study

CHRISTIAN REFORMED HOME MISSIONS, 2850 Kalamazoo Ave., S.E., Grand Rapids, MI 49560 (616-246-0772).

*Coffee Break Evangelism.* Women's outreach Bible studies designed to reach unchurched women in the community.

*Men's Life Bible Study.* A seven-week series designed for men's groups.

*Discover Your Bible Series.* Church-oriented inductive Bible studies from a Reformed perspective.

CHURCHES ALIVE, Box 3800, San Bernardino, CA 92413 (714-886-5361).

*God in You Bible Study Series*

FISHERMAN BIBLE STUDYGUIDES published by Harold Shaw Publishers, Box 567, Wheaton, IL 60189 (708-665-6700). Inductive studies for use by neighborhood, student, and church groups. Titles include Bible book studies (all New Testament books and nine Old Testament books), topical studies, and character studies. Several titles for evangelistic Bible studies are available.

Other series from Harold Shaw Publishers:

NETWORK BIBLE STUDIES. Contemporary issues for "people on the move." Specifically designed for marketplace studies, these studies are designed to be completed in thirty minutes. They can also be used in home or church groups.

YOUNG FISHERMAN BIBLE STUDYGUIDES. Inductive studies for teens, including book studies, character studies, outreach studies, and topical studies. Separate leader and student guides.

SHAW BIBLE DISCOVERY GUIDES FOR CAMPERS. Inductive studies specifically written for camp settings. Includes six titles for junior campers and six titles for teen campers based on relational, interactive topics suited to camp life.

LIFEGUIDE BIBLE STUDY SERIES published by InterVarsity Press, Box F, Downers Grove, IL 60515 (708-964-5700). Inductive Bible study guides on books of the Bible and topical studies. Studies are designed to be completed in forty-five minutes and include leader's helps in each book.

LIFECHANGE BIBLE STUDY SERIES published by NavPress (NAVIGATORS), P.O. Box 6000, Colorado Springs, CO 80934 (800-525-7151). Bible book studies with extensive background notes and leader's helps. Designed to be completed in one hour, with one hour at-home preparation.

NEIGHBORHOOD BIBLE STUDIES published by Tyndale, P.O. Box 80, Wheaton, IL 60189 (708-668-8300). Inductive Bible studies especially geared for outreach groups. Guides have been translated into over thirty languages, including a simple-English guide. Information available from Neighborhood Bible Studies, Box 222, Dobbs Ferry, NY 10522 (914-693-3273).

SERENDIPITY, Box 1012, Littleton, CO 80160 (800-525-9563). Series include:

MASTERING THE BASICS. In-depth Bible courses for home groups combining personal, small group, and large group elements.

SUPPORT GROUP SERIES. Topical studies primarily designed for Baby Boomers with basic and in-depth tracks.

YOUTH BIBLE STUDY SERIES. Studies and interactive activities for teens.

SERENDIPITY BIBLE FOR GROUPS. Features the NIV text with questions for group study in the margins.

WORKSHOP BIBLE STUDY SERIES published by Zondervan Publishers, 1415 Lake Drive, S.E. Grand Rapids, MI 549506 (800-824-5280). Series includes Bible book and topical studies with leader's notes and suggestions for at-home study through the week.

## Journals and Newsletters

*Christian Education Journal* published by Scripture Press Ministries, P.O. Box 650, Glen Ellyn, IL 60138. A journal designed to promote growth and advancement in the field of Christian education; often includes articles about small group ministries and Christian community.

*Leadership*, a practical journal for church leaders published by Christianity Today, Inc. which often addresses issues related to small groups. Subscription service: 465 Gundersen Dr., Carol Stream, IL 60188.

"The Small Group Letter," a newsletter for small group leaders which appears as an insert in *Discipleship Journal* published by the Navigators. For subscriptions, write to P.O. Box 54470, Boulder, CO 80323.

## Resource Organizations

Neighborhood Bible Studies, Inc. provides seminars, materials, and yearly conferences on outreach Bible studies. For information write to: Box 222, Dobbs Ferry, NY 10522 (914-693-3273).

Serendipity Seminars provide training in developing and leading small groups. For information write to: Box 11012, Littleton, CO 80160 (800-525-9563).

Stephen Ministries trains lay people for caring ministries in the church. For information, write to: 1325 Boland, St. Louis, MO 63117 (314-645-5511).

# Index